Marketplace Mentality

How to develop the core beliefs required for global dominion in the marketplace.

Dr. Victor S. Couzens, Sr.

xulon
PRESS

Copyright © 2013 by Dr. Victor S. Couzens, Sr.

Marketplace Mentality
How to develop the core beliefs required for global dominion in the marketplace.
by Dr. Victor S. Couzens, Sr.

Printed in the United States of America

ISBN 9781628398786

All rights reserved solely by the author. The author guarantees all contents are original and do not infringe upon the legal rights of any other person or work. No part of this book may be reproduced in any form without the permission of the author. The views expressed in this book are not necessarily those of the publisher.

Unless otherwise indicated, Bible quotations are taken from the New International Version (NIV). Copyright © 1973, 1978, 1984, 2011 by Biblica, Inc.™. Used by permission. All rights reserved.

www.xulonpress.com

Dedication

I dedicate this, my first book, to my maternal grandmother Cassie Mae Couzens and my paternal grandmother Flora Yvonne Taylor. It was in their faith that the first fruit of my own faith was cultivated.

High Praise for Dr. Victor Couzens and the book, Marketplace Mentality

"Bishop Victor Couzens' insight and passion to reach people both within and outside the Church leap from the pages of this dynamic work. In these pages you will find a fresh perspective, a clear process to engage business and Kingdom principles, and encouragement to make a difference right where you are now. Read this book and watch your business and ministry launch to a higher level."

Rev. Dr. Stephen and Kellie Swisher
Senior Executives
Kenneth Copeland Ministries
Ft. Worth, Texas

"Dr. Couzens raises the bar with his evocative and yet practical teaching in Marketplace Mentality. Each chapter will take you to a familiar place in the biblical story and open a new door for your living as a faithful follower of Jesus".

Rev. Dr. Duane A Anders
Senior Pastor Cathedral of the Rockies United Methodist
Church, Boise ID

"Bishop Couzens has made the word so direct and concise. As young professionals, our talents are often used outside of the church and we are not in the spotlight within the Church. However, as the mission of the Church expands outside of four walls, our skill set and talents allow us to maximize those for the benefit of the Church. In other words, just because we are not behind the microphone in a robe, doesn't limit our ability to further and strengthen the mission of the Church."

Jason & Tiffany Dunn CRNA

Acknowledgements

Truly, I could fill an entire book thanking the innumerable people who have mentored, encouraged, influenced, challenged and contributed to Marketplace Mentality in some way. It is true, we are the sum total of the experiences we have and the people we encounter.

I would like to personally acknowledge the ministry partners of Inspirational Baptist Church–City of Destiny. May God bless you for encouraging me to reach the masses for the cause of Christ. Thank you.

To my executive administrator Tracy Lee, my administrative assistant Demecia Jett, my media director and graphic designer Gregory Lee and my writing assistant Lois Smith; Words cannot express how critically important and valuable you have been at every stage of this book! There's a special place for each of you in the kingdom.

Last, but not least my children: Faith, Victor II, Daija, Trinity, Jameison and Charity. THANK YOU for always helping Daddy remember what's most important! I love each of you entirely.

Table of Contents

Preface xiii

Chapter One – The Marketplace. 15
Chapter Two – Marketplace Mentality and The Kingdom 25
Chapter Three – This Is How We Do It 35
Chapter Four – Renewing Your Mind – The Mission is HIS. 41
Chapter Five – Purposed By Design 49
Chapter Six – You Are Anointed 59
Chapter Seven – The No Compromise Zone 67
Chapter Eight – Release Your Influence 77
Chapter Nine – Yes, It's Personal 89
Chapter Ten – God Speaks. 95

Preface

"Christianity means a lot more than church membership."[1]
— Billy Sunday

In this fast paced, technological world that we live in, it is easy to see yourself as insignificant and of no consequence in what is the greatest agenda known to mankind: **advancing the Kingdom of God**. No matter how much the Internet is developed, no matter what the latest app is for the smartphone, no matter how huge social media sites become or whatever the latest tech gadget or gizmo is, one thing remains true. God uses every day, ordinary people to continue to increase His Kingdom here on earth.

When Jesus spoke the words, "The Kingdom of God is like..." (Mark 4:26), He was establishing a priority that believers, both then and to come, would operate in the Marketplace.

Therefore, a particular set of core beliefs must govern the life of those who are intent on leaving a mark on this earth that cannot be erased. If you are reading this book, it's because you are such a person — you have an awareness that a unique spiritual DNA lives inside of you. Whether you recognize it or not YOU are a vital part of the movement

> *"...the greatest agenda known to mankind—advancing the **Kingdom of God**..."*

that started thousands of years ago of advancing God's Kingdom on earth. **Marketplace Mentality** is not a "how to" book, it is a "how not to" book—how not to miss your role in God's corporate agenda. This is done by renewing your core beliefs, thought process, reshaping your mentality and surrendering your every ability to the purpose of God.

Do you remember an explorer by the name of Jacques Cousteau? Cousteau was an explorer from France who set out on unusual expeditions. Jacques Cousteau sailed the seas, searching the bottom of the oceans looking for relics left behind from pirate's ships and the like. Cousteau was on a mission not of discovery, but on a mission of restoration to reclaim those treasures that had been lost.

In that same vein, I write this book *Marketplace Mentality* to renew the hearts and the minds of God's people concerning how we view ourselves in the world. The goal of this book is to re-establish the believer's need for the power and strength of God's word. This is the strength required to reclaim your place on the earth as an agent of change and influence for Kingdom of the Lord.

Chapter One

The Marketplace

What do we mean by marketplace? According to the Merriam-Webster Dictionary, the definition of marketplace is "the world of trade or economic activity: the everyday world."[2] This would be the believer's workplace, career, vocation and other areas of influence. Notice I did not use the word jobs. Believers don't have jobs, they have marketplace assignments. These are the areas of your life where you have presence and influence, whether you are a stay-at-home parent or the CEO of a major conglomerate.

God is strategically salting the earth with believers that are scattered throughout the world to establish His principles in every area of life. It has been the mindset of some believers that their role in furthering the Kingdom is relegated to what we do in the local church, e.g.–a deacon, a Sunday school teacher or an usher. However, if that was the only role God was interested in, He would have made every day Sunday thereby eliminating any need for believers to function in another assignment.

Jesus said, "You are the salt of the earth...You are the light of the world..." (Matt. 5:13-14). Life is more than church on Sunday. Each church assignment is significant; and yet each is simply a CATALYST to expand the Kingdom of God and not a plateau.

If we are going to possess the marketplace mentality we must be careful to not shun, but have an appreciation for words like "post-modernism," "crossover" and "secularism." Each of these provides a window into the worldview of mainstream culture.

Post-modernism is, in brief, a set of ideas or core beliefs that denies the existence of absolute truth. Truth from a post-modern perspective is relative and self-defined, so much so that it is impossible to give a concrete definition of post-modernism. It is only possible to describe or explain, but not define. Post-modernists would certainly shudder at being defined. They prefer to not be strongly identified with a particular line of thought.

Similar to post-modernism, secularism is a way of thinking which is void of authority. It is built on the personal philosophy of the individual. Void of God, the supernatural and religion in general, secularism regards the temporal and the carnal above all else.

Crossover is often the phrase used to describe something that has its influence in one market and yet appeals to more than one market. This term is used in many industries from automotive to music. It has been unnecessarily met with significant consternation in Christian culture. However, unlike post-modernism and secularism, crossover is an underused tool in the mandate to penetrate the earth with the culture and influence of the Kingdom.

The song "O, Happy Day" recorded by the Edwin Hawkins singers in 1970 was the first gospel song to crossover to secular charts. The song not only sold millions but, by being played on secular radio stations and ranking highly on secular charts, it exposed millions of people to the message and love of Christ. The Kingdom needs this type of influence.

In recent years we have seen this same crossover appeal not only with Christian music, but also with the message of Christ in books like *The Purpose Driven Life*, in movies like *The Passion of The Christ*, in television

The Marketplace

shows like *Touched By An Angel* and *The Bible (mini-series)*. More people watched the mini-series *The Bible* than reality television during the five weeks it aired. Although the technique may change, the message of the Kingdom remains the same.

Operating out of an overly-religious mindset will often cause us not to see that the Kingdom is actually contained and not advanced if we lack crossover appeal. Having crossover appeal must be viewed as a new way of believing. It must be appreciated as a type of 'overt conspiracy' to influence the earth for the cause of the Kingdom.

Although we are suggesting a paradigm shift, it is important to recognize that a new system of beliefs is not required for believers to do as they have been called to do; dominate (Gen. 1:28). The Lord intends for believers to be headlights, not taillights. We lead the way!

The six core beliefs that will be identified in the book to help us establish our *Marketplace Mentality* may be explained differently and with another measure of revelation, however what is required for believers to dominate is "a new way of believing, not simply new answers to the same old questions but a new set of questions."[3]

These new questions must challenge our traditional view of discipleship, media, arts and entertainment, family, government, religion, business and education. Questions like:

"Why is there a separation between church and state?"
"Who stole the voice of Christ in mainstream society?"
"What does it really mean to be the salt of the earth and the light of the world?"
"Why are we consumed with sins from the waist down only?"
"Do boundaries really exist?"
"What is the responsibility of believers to people of other faiths or no faith at all?"
"Is the mission of Christ still relevant?"

The probing and response to these questions on a personal level activates a mission of renewal and opens up the heart to receive a new way of believing. This new way of believing is called a *marketplace mentality*.

Think about this. Our galaxy, the Milky Way, consists of eight planets. Our planet Earth has more than seven billion people; yet believers are the critical agents chosen to not only impact, but dominate this vast topography. It has been the plan of God from the beginning that His own would have dominion over the earth (Gen. 1:28).

It takes more than a single grain of salt to flavor food and if a light source is turned on, it is impossible to contain it; it gives light to the entire area. As the salt of the earth and the light of the world, our collective influence as believers in Jesus Christ should have the same effect.

In our marketplace assignments we must be yielded to be used by the Lord, to be an example and model of integrity, commitment, peace, courage, excellence, cooperation, humility and grace. Those who approach their assignments with these virtues bring honor to God and advance His Kingdom.

With this in mind, God has given each of us spheres of influence to be realized in every area of part of the earth and corner of the world. As an illustration of this fact, in 1975 God gave a vision to Bill Bright (founder of Campus Crusade for Christ), to Loren Cunningham (founder of Youth with a Mission), and to noted author and theologian Frances Schaeffer.[4] These three men conferred, and agreed that God was revealing to each a separate, particular part of the same vision regarding the *"seven mountains of influence"*.

They came together, each submitting the part of the vision they had in order to get a full understanding. What God revealed to them was if Christians were in leadership of these seven mountains that the world would be transformed into a place that reflected practices and principles based upon the mind of God.

The Marketplace

The mountains are identified as: Religion, Arts and Entertainment, Education, Government, Family, Media and Finance. These men embraced this mandate from God, and began to see themselves as "Change Agents." Renowned pastor Dr. Bill Winston states this: "We [Christians] should be the problem solvers for this time. We were not created to run from problems, we run to them. Why? Because we have an answer to every problem in the world."[5]

Renowned teacher and theologian Lance Wallnau has several teachings based on the "Revelation of the Seven Mountains."[5] Wallnau states that one of the reasons for the decay of society is that Christians are not in places of great influence on the seven mountains. He asserts that this world would be in more redemptive if Christians were in positions of power on these seven mountains, because faith would dictate the decisions. I believe this to be true. When decisions are enacted on the mountains, everything in the valley (marketplace) as a whole is affected then for the cause of Christ. Dr. Cornel West states it this way, "You've got to be a thermostat rather than a thermometer. A thermostat shapes the climate of opinion; a thermometer just reflects it."[7]

Although neither Bright, Cunningham, Schaeffer nor Wallnau has stated such, I believe that there is direct evidence in the Word of God to support the vision of the seven mountains.

We read in Isaiah 11:1-3, "A shoot will come up from the stump of Jesse; from his roots a Branch will bear fruit. The Spirit of the LORD will rest on him— the Spirit of wisdom and of understanding, the Spirit of counsel and of power, the Spirit of knowledge and of the fear of the LORD—and he will delight in the fear of the LORD."

The overarching principle we see in this passage is although He was present in eternity, the coming Messiah ascended to earth to establish the Kingdom age. The prophecy of this passage in Isaiah points to His literal and spiritual manifestation on the earth. John reminds us of the eternal reality of Christ by writing, in John 1, "In the beginning was the Word, and the Word was with God, and the Word was God. ²He was with God in the beginning. ³Through him all things were made; without him nothing was made that has been made."

We understand then that the entire world was made through the Branch from the root of Jesse and that the Spirit of the Lord rested upon Him. We see this in Isaiah 11; we have Jesus, the Spirit and the Lord; that's the Father, the Son and the Holy Spirit – on which all of the earth is established and out of that foundation come seven spirits or mountains of influence.

We have experienced a subtle shift in our world. Arts and Entertainment were once a reflection of the values and morals society holds. However, what was once considered behavior that fell outside of society's standards quickly has become more commonplace and depicted in the Arts and Entertainment industry. Isaiah 11:2 says, "The Spirit of the LORD will rest on him." In order for there to be a return to Biblical values, we know that the Spirit of the Lord must rest (abide, stay, influence, and remain). Nowhere is that more apparent than in Arts and Entertainment which is a calibrator the worldview of society.

The Spirit of wisdom is mirrored in the field of education. Wisdom in its purest sense is defined as applied knowledge. A society rests on the strength of its educational system or mountain, knowing that every citizen of that society is a product of that society's education. It would be quite logical, then to make the connection of Godly educators resulting in a more Godly society.

The Media Mountain – television, radio, newspaper, the internet and more – are information resources or vehicles that people use to gain understanding of their world . We rely on media outlets to relay to us what is happening in our world, whether it is down the street or on the other side of the world. With the rise of the internet and digital

The Marketplace

technologies, the speed at which that information is shared is faster than ever. In the passage in Isaiah, we see the Mountain of Media as needing to be dominated by the Spirit of understanding.

The Spirit of counsel is represented in the Mountain of Family. Whether functional or dysfunctional, if you lived with your immediate or extended family, whether your growing up years were great or you experienced some challenges—the family is where your formative values are shaped. It is where you learn to interact with the world and with others, family is where your purpose is defined, and often the place you return to for wisdom and counsel. What you experience, what you grow up with becomes your standard for the world, and every decision you make is in some way vetted by the counsel of family.

> *"It is God's desire that we think beyond 'church' as the only thing we consider to be Kingdom."*

Still in Isaiah 11:2, the next Spirit that is mentioned is the Mountain of Might. Might is defined as the power, authority, or resources wielded (as by an individual or group). This mountain is represented in government. In government we have three branches (or sources of might, if you will), legislative, judicial and executive. To clarify, let's use the illustration of a police officer. There is inherent power in a man or a woman being a police officer because of the authority of the entity they represent. The Greek word for this type of power is kratos. The minute a man or woman takes the oath and becomes an officer, they have power. Why? Because of exousia (gr.)—the power of rule or government (the power of him whose will and commands must be submitted to by others and obeyed universally). The government has given them authority to make and keep the peace, many times for that to happen all a police officer really has to do is show up in uniform. A police officer also has dunamis (gr.)– which is defined as inherent power, power residing in a thing by virtue of its nature, or which a person or thing exerts and puts forth. Should exousia and kratos not be sufficient, on the officer's hip rests the dunamis needed to keep peace.

Isaiah 11:2 speaks of the Spirit of knowledge. This relates to the Finance Mountain. Money is a tool that speaks the universal language of power and influence. In our global economy, it is imperative to have expertise in financial matters in order to use money as effectively as possible for the advancement of the Kingdom.

The last Spirit mentioned in Isaiah 11:2 is "the fear of the LORD." This "fear" of the LORD is actually reverence, awe and deference. We learn these things concerning the LORD from the Mountain of Religion. The mountain religion is so important that Isaiah says in 11:3 that true happiness begins with a reverence for God.

It is important to note that religion is just one of the mountains of influence. Why, you may ask? You ask great questions. The reason why it is important to note that religion is just one of the mountains is to gain the proper perspective of the organized church's role in the world.

This revelation reminds us is that while we gather throughout the week in local congregations to worship God and study His Word; this is only one segment of our lives. I believe it is God's desire that we begin to look beyond church as the one segment of time in our week that we are focusing on God. We need to operate from a more integrative, holistic thought pattern that intertwines our faith into everything that we do. It is true; people of faith should assemble in the house of God for teaching, worship and fellowship. All of these things develop Christ-like character. Yet, as our mindsets are transformed, our efforts should reflect the teaching of our faith on the other six days of the week. The entire purpose of the Mountain of Religion experience inside is to empower believers to work the other six Mountains.

As the salt of the earth and the light of the world we are to bring forth the transformative power of our Word and Worship experiences on the Mountain of Religion and not compartmentalize our responsibility in Christ to an experience on but on Sunday only. We are to take the impartation received from the Word and Worship into our marketplace assignments.

Doing this causes us to operate and think by the standards of which Jesus taught. This level of thinking is what we call a "marketplace mentality."

Chapter Two

Marketplace Mentality and the Kingdom

The sin of Adam in Eden disrupted the original design of the Kingdom. Adam had all of the joy of the Kingdom; uninterrupted fellowship with God. He had the influence of Kingdom dominion; he named every animal in Eden. He had the resources needed to manage the Kingdom; the rivers and the vegetation were under his dominion and at his disposal. He had faith; He enjoyed the presence of God. Even the qualities of Adam's core beliefs were reminiscent of the Kingdom. He had no shame or ill feelings concerning nakedness. It was only after he subjugated his influence to the enemy that he had to toil to manifest resources and the quality of his core beliefs became inferior. *Adam, in his sin, negotiated away the right of his dominion and the impact of His influence over every aspect of the kingdom.* He and all of humanity to follow would now require an intermediary, a redeemer and a restorer.

Ironically, Satan tried to negotiate the Kingdoms back to God. Matthew 4:8 reads, "Again, the devil took Him up on a very high mountain and showed Him all the kingdoms of the world and the glory (the splendor, magnificence, preeminence, and excellence) of them. And he said to Him, These things, all taken together, I will give You, if You will prostrate Yourself before me and do homage *and* worship me" (AMP).

Through His death, burial and resurrection Christ ransomed the Kingdom back. "The Kingdom suffereth violence and the violent take it by force" (Matt. 11:19, KJV).

The influence that Adam lost Christ restored, but most believers have not fully assimilated the right of influence and dominion concerning the Kingdom. Hear the words of Christ in Matthew 16:19, "I will give you the keys of the kingdom of heaven; whatever you bind on earth will be bound in heaven, and whatever you loose on earth will be loosed in heaven." (Do you hear the level of influence and dominion we have been given?!)

Christ left for the believer the dominion to permit and prohibit on earth on behalf of the Kingdom. Christ is blatantly clear about His mission: restore the Kingdom. In fact He had one message, and it was and is the message of the Kingdom.

The first public sermon of Christ concerned the Kingdom: "And saying, Repent (think differently; change your mind, regretting your sins and changing your conduct), for the kingdom of heaven is at hand" (Matt 3:2, AMP). Furthermore He proclaims, "And this good news of the kingdom (the Gospel) will be preached throughout the whole world as a testimony to all the nations" (Matt. 24:14, AMP).

These two passages are arguably bookends in the ministry of Christ concerning the Kingdom. The strategic manner of His activity between these above mentioned texts further affirms the mandate of restoring Kingdom dominion. Even the Old Testament speaks of the mission of Christ to restore and advance the Kingdom. Isaiah 9:6-7 says, "And the government shall be upon His shoulder...Of the increase of His government and of peace there shall be no end, upon the throne of David and over his Kingdom, to establish it and to uphold it with justice and with righteousness from the (latter) time forth, even forevermore."

Let us be clear that the word *government* means rule and or dominion. Thus, the mission of the Messiah was not to only redeem our souls from sin, it was equally to use His influence to reestablish and rule the government consistent with God's standard of righteousness. Critical to the success of His mission is the renewing of the minds of the citizens of the Kingdom. How we view influence, dominion, authority, accountability and involvement requires the maintenance and washing of the Word.

For years many believers' minds have long been bent toward religion and religion only! While we are correct to focus on the cultivating of our faith, our revelation is incomplete if faith is all we endeavor to cultivate. We have an equal obligation to cultivate our gifts, maximize our connections and seek opportunities to broaden our influence and impact. We are admonished of such in Jeremiah 48:10 states, "Cursed be he who does the work of the Lord negligently (with slackness, deceitfully)..." (AMP). Believers have an obligation to be prudent and diligent in every way and over every resource.

Some have ignorantly denounced wealth and influence among believers. We need our minds renewed if we believe having t such tools is unrighteous... Hear the mind of God concerning wealth and influence. "The wealth of the wicked is laid up for the righteous" (Prov. 13:22, KJV). Another passage says, "He may prepare it, but the just will wear it, and the innocent will divide the silver" (Job 27:17, AMP). *He* in this text refers to the wicked. The Kingdom is a major force and it demands every resource on every level for the cause of Christ. This includes people resources, financial resources and the influence to negotiate positive change.

Learning to interpret our worldview from the perspective of being a disciple doesn't only mean that you are born again. Coming into the Kingdom means that you see and submit your entire life to the Lordship of Jesus Christ. You – yes you—have a singular role in God's corporate agenda, and it is God's agenda to bring all of humanity under the authority of the Kingdom.

To come under the authority of the Kingdom of Christ is to be His disciple. Embrace that God has given you a singular role of bringing others into the Kingdom. He has a plan to disperse you strategically across the mountains of influence to fulfill His agenda.

To come into the Kingdom is to be a part of the society of God. *Basileia is* the Greek word for the society of His rule, authority, dominion, and reign. It can be somewhat intimidating in this big ole world to imagine how you, as one person, could possibly have an impact or be a part of what God is doing. Nevertheless, it is so important that we all remember that every door swings on a hinge. You don't pay attention to the hinge; all the attention is set on a door. You may not be the door, but certainly you are a hinge. God is using you to make things happen in the world and mountains of Arts and Entertainment, Education, Media, Family, Government, Finance and Religion.

There's something very specific that God endeavors for you to do on His agenda. So we are clear, let us consider more fully exactly what God's agenda is. God's agenda is so important that He has not left it to us to try and figure it out. This does not require figuring out; it only requires a more prayerful consideration of the scriptures. The scriptures declare quite emphatically what His agenda is.

In I Timothy 2:3 (AMP), the Word says, "³ For such [praying] is good *and* right, and [it is] pleasing *and* acceptable to God our Savior..." verse 4, "Who wishes (speaking of God, God wishes) all *men to be saved and [increasingly] to perceive and* recognize *and* discern *and* know precisely *and* correctly the [divine] Truth" (italics mine). Hold that in mind.

Consider Matthew 28:19. Matthew 28:19 says, "¹⁹ Go then and make disciples of all the nations, baptizing them into the name of the Father and of the Son and of the Holy Spirit." Now II Peter 3:9 says, "⁹

The Lord does not delay *and* is not tardy *or* slow about what He promises, according to some people's conception of slowness, but He is long-suffering (extraordinarily patient) toward you, not desiring that any should perish, but that all should turn to repentance" (AMP). Peter says that the Lord has not delayed His coming just for the sake of delaying it, but the Lord delaying His coming is a part of His strategic plan. He has strategically not come back, because by Him not coming back yet, others are given the opportunity to come to Him through repentance.

When we look at Matthew 28:19, I Timothy 2 and II Peter 3:9 side by side we can clearly see what God's agenda is. Part of God's strategy is to fulfill His agenda is to by using disciples to make disciples, using influencers to develop influencers, using change agents to develop change agents. Karl Barth says, "The call issued by Jesus is a call to discipleship."[9]

Everyone has an assignment. Look in the mirror and tell yourself, "I have an assignment." Everyone has a spiritual gift. Look again and say, "I have a spiritual gift." Now here's what you want to understand, all gifts and all assignments are for the Kingdom, but all gifts and all assignments won't be executed in a church environment. This means that just because your assignment may not come with a platform or a microphone -just because your assignment may not put you up under lights doesn't mean that your assignment is any less significant as it relates to bringing others into the Kingdom.

> *"God's agenda is to bring all of humanity into the Kingdom by using believers in the marketplace."*

So, you may ask, "Dr. Couzens, how do I identify my assignment?" I'm glad you asked, keep asking good questions. God has uniquely designed us so that our assignment correlates with our natural ability and spiritual gifts. There is no disconnect, instead there is a crossover between my natural ability and my assignment for the marketplace. Consider Jeremiah 1:5, "Before I formed you in the womb I knew [and] approved of you [as My chosen instrument], and before you were born I separated *and* set you apart, consecrating you; [and] I appointed you as a prophet to the nations" (AMP).

At birth you had all the raw material you would ever need to complete your assignment, both natural and spiritual. God *knew* you, inside and out, before you took your first breath and He had already determined the plan for your life, including your marketplace assignment. His desire is to use you to increase His Kingdom wherever you are and in whatever capacity you serve.

This may sound unusual coming from a preacher, but God is bigger than any one platform, including being called to preach. God needs disciples in the operating room. God needs disciples in the courthouse. God needs disciples in government. God needs disciples in banking. God needs disciples in insurance. God needs disciples in education. God needs disciples in the military. Though your gift may not show up on the stage at church, it does not mean that your gift is not a significant part of advancing the Kingdom.

In the preface of this book, I mentioned that we would be examining the thought patterns and core beliefs that are necessary in developing a marketplace mentality. *Core belief #1 –* The Kingdom is more than the church. Let's look at a Biblical example of being called to be used for the Kingdom in unconventional way

Something very interesting happens in Mark chapter 5. In Mark 5, the Lord delivers a man that had been mentally unstable. The Bible says the man was tormented by demonic forces. In short, The Lord sends the demons into the pigs and the pigs go over the hill. But, check this out— keep in mind again that it's all gifts and callings are for the Kingdom, but they won't all be executed in the church.

Mark 5:18, "And when He had stepped into the boat, [this is Jesus. Jesus is getting in the boat, he's leaving so] the man who had been controlled by the unclean spirits kept begging Him that he might be with Him" (AMP). That's a noble thing. The man wants to go with Jesus. But something interesting happens here. The Bible says, "But Jesus refused to permit him..." Hold on, push pause. I personally initially experienced theological tension when I read this. This is the same Jesus that got upset at another place in the gospel because half of the disciples turned and left Him. Now He's got a man who wants to go with Him, and He's says, "No, you can't go with me." No?! What kind of thing is this?

> *"To be a disciple is to be an adherent to the teachings of another. You are a disciple of whoever shapes your core beliefs."*

I thought Jesus wanted people to follow Him. Why can't the man go with Jesus? What Is He doing? Jesus is breaking this man's one-mountain mentality. This man passionately wants to be used in a way that though honorable, would actually contain his influence and ability to dominate. He sees the mountain of religion as the place to be, however, the Lord has another plan. He must have a marketplace mentality in order to cultivate the raw material in him.

When you read through the scripture, you see all kinds of people that Jesus used, but their assignments were not always executed in the temple. Yet, they were still used by God. The wise men in Matthew 2, they were trained in Astronomy, they were scientists, they knew how to read the stars. Luke who wrote the gospel of Luke and Acts...He wasn't a prophet, he wasn't a priest, he was just an ordinary Doctor that loved Jesus. Jesus' earthly father Joseph was a carpenter. Joseph could hook up a bird tree, a coffee table, two end tables and an entertainment system in a weekend. There was an Ethiopian eunuch in Acts 8 who was the Chairman of the

Federal Reserve for Kandake; Benaniah in I Chronicles 11 that King David's Director of Homeland Security. These are just a few examples of various mountains being dominated by the people of God.

Back to Mark 5, this man wants to go with Jesus and Jesus says, "No, you can't go with me, because the assignment I have for you doesn't involve you sitting on the backside of a mountain with me." I have called you to be a missionary. If you really want to maximize the abilities I have given you, don't get on this boat and go with me. Go home."

It's amazing how people want to be used of God in church, but are not as excited about being used of God at home or on other mountains. Jesus said to the man, "You can't go with me, go home. And when you get home, tell everybody what I have done for you

Remember, it's all for the Kingdom, but not all executed in the church. Mark 5, verse 20 reads, "And he departed and began to publicly proclaim in Decapolis [the region of the ten cities]..." This man desperately wanted to go with Jesus. Jesus says, "No." This man had no awareness that by the Lord sending him home he was positioning him to wield more influence than he would ever have imagined. The Lord was setting him up to dominate his city for the cause of the Kingdom

In effect Jesus says, "Do you want to argue over who is going to lead the next song in the choir or do you want me to release you as a Missionary to go to foreign countries? Do you want to sit up in church and fight over a seat, or do you want me to send you into the hedges and highways and compel others to come?" Now granted, as a believer you need the church and you are the church. You are the church in your marketplace assignment, in your neighborhood, in Arts and Entertainment, Education, Media, Family, Government, Finance *and* Religion.

Let's bring some life application to this text. "Do you want your name called because of your macaroni salad or do you want me to show you how to feed thousands of homeless people?" This is the impact of Jesus question." Now, consider Mark 7. This renewed my mind when the Holy Ghost gave me this revelation.

Keep in mind this now delivered man understandably wanted to go with Jesus and Jesus denies his request letting him know that accompanying Him was not his assignment. His assignment was to go home. Mark 7:31, "Soon after this, Jesus, coming back from the region of Tyre, passed through Sidon on to the Sea of Galilee, through the region of [where?] Decapolis [the ten cities]" (AMP). Jesus is back in this man's territory now.

Now consider Mark 8:1. Jesus is in Decapolis, the formerly demon possessed man has now become a type of overseer of ten cities. Mark 8:1, "In those days when [again] an immense crowd had gathered..." (AMP). Don't miss this. Jesus is in Decapolis. He sent the man to be a missionary in Decapolis. When Jesus comes back to Decapolis, this man had cultivated his assignment to the extent of dominion. The Bible records that there were 5,000 men plus women and children gathered personally to hear the Lord. This is the place where Jesus used a little boy's lunch of two fish and five pieces of bread and fed the multitude; that happened in Decapolis. The people undoubtedly were gathered there in part because this one man was faithful to his assignment. He had renewed his mind to the extent that a marketplace mentality had developed.

All God needs you to do are the things He called you to do.

It may not be glamorous, it may not come with a big light, nobody may ever know your name, but if you just work the mountains has called you the world will be a more redemptive place. The Kingdom of God will spread closer to the edges of the earth, and every mountain will be dominated for the glory of God.

You have a gift, you have a talent, and you have ability that when paired with a marketplace mentality places you in the impenetrable force of the change agents. As you activate your marketplace mentality, watch God take you from grace to grace and from glory to glory.

Chapter Three

This Is How We Do It

Just as a child of a United States citizen who is born in France is both a French citizen and a citizen of the United States,[10] so are those who confess Jesus Christ as Lord. Because of our alignment with Christ, we maintain dual citizenship between heaven and earth. There are precepts, guidelines and laws that we must follow as citizens in order to effectively fulfill our assignment, both in the natural realm and the spiritual realm. Believers are expected to operate not only as citizens of the Kingdom of God, but equally as citizens of God who live on the earth.

> *"Marketplace Mentality is a level of thinking that causes believers to reclaim the inheritance of influence and dominion in every Kingdom of the earth."*

As citizens of both the Kingdom of God and the earth, we have rights and responsibilities. We understand that there are laws that govern society to maintain order, and the same is true for the Kingdom of God. Simply put, <u>marketplace mentality is the way in which we allow our thinking to be renewed to the extent that it positively enhances our understanding of the global and diverse dimensions of the role of the believer in the earth.</u>

Remember earlier we mentioned Matthew 5:13-16:

> "You are the salt of the earth. But if the salt loses its saltiness, how can it be made salty again? It is no longer good for anything, except to be thrown out and trampled underfoot. You are the light of the world. A town built on a hill cannot be hidden. Neither do people light a lamp and put it under a bowl. Instead they put it on its stand, and it gives light to everyone in the house. In the same way, let your light shine before others, that they may see your good deeds and glorify your Father in heaven."

Let's dig a little deeper into this text. One of the qualities of salt is that it preserves. As Christ's disciples, believers are the preservative agents of the will and mind of God in the earth. Light illuminates and reveals. As light, believers are to make known the concerns and priorities of our Lord so that others can experience the authority and compassion of God. We are admonished by Christ to do these things in a marketplace fashion, out in the open—not hidden—so that God is glorified and all things are reconciled back into His kingdom. God has strategically deposited specific abilities in you for the express purpose of taking back the influence of His Kingdom.

There is a passage in Colossians that speaks to this point. Please do not get frustrated if you feel like God's not using you in your local church or in ways of your own interests or design. There are multiplicities of needs in the earth that can only be best served by believers.

Colossians 3:23 says: "Whatever may be your task, work at it heartily (from the soul), as [something done] for the Lord and not for men."(AMP)

In reshaping and renewing our mentality, we must view each and every assignment as a platform to glorify Christ, redeem the earth and advance the Kingdom. Whichever mountain your task(s) falls upon (i.e.

family, education, media, finance, government, etc.) appreciate it as a sovereign opportunity from the Lord.

How are we to do what we do? We are to do it with an attitude of appreciation, even if the task itself cuts against your own desire or the desire of others for your life.

To help us further develop our marketplace mentality, let's examine the revelation we find in Jeremiah 1. Jeremiah 1:1 says, "The words of Jeremiah son of Hilkiah, one of the *priests* at Anathoth in the territory of Benjamin..." (Italics mine).

This is a tremendous observation. Although Jeremiah was born into a family of priests and God says to him (paraphrase), "I didn't ordain you to be a priest, I ordained you to be a prophet." One truth that this text tells us is that you can't always tell what your assignment is by looking at your family. Neither can you dismiss your assignment because it does not parallel the assignment of others in your family. Yes, we can easily name families that have generations of preachers, teacher, athletes, attorneys, etc. However, God may have a different plan for your life. Whatever His plan for your life is, appreciate it!

In the Old Testament, the priests went before the Lord on behalf of the people. The prophet went before the people on behalf of the Lord. Another truth we find in the first chapter of Jeremiah is that Jeremiah was sure of his calling, he was sure of his assignment, but he was never happy in it. He never had joy in it. He knew what he was supposed to be doing, what God had anointed him to do, but he wasn't ever really excited about it. Neither did he appreciate it. Yet, God did not remove the burden of His mission for Jeremiah. This is why you should avoid using your feelings as a barometer regarding your assignment.

If you recognize you have been struggling to accept God's assignment, refuse to allow the enemy to bring you into condemnation. Just purpose to fully develop a God honoring attitude about how He wants to use you and ask the Lord to renew your mentality to that which is more appreciative.

Jeremiah spent a considerable amount of time complaining. This was not subtle complaining either—often He complained aloud to God, "Why did you put this on me? You have made me the laughingstock of all of Israel." He didn't even like the people he had to work with...imagine that -not liking the people you have to work with or work for. Jeremiah 11 and Jeremiah 12 recount his attitude concerning this.

It is important that we understand that everybody God used in the Bible did not act like the Magi who risked their lives to confirm the birth of the Messiah. Not everybody embraced their mission or leapt with joy and sang, *"If the Lord needs somebody, send me. If the Lord needs somebody, I'll go."* No, everybody in the Bible didn't respond like that. In fact, many people in the Bible, when they understood the call of God, attempted to run from it or got down right angry with God. There's a powerful revelation here, though; I need to give this to you. Let's look at Jeremiah 15; you've got to see this for yourself.

Jeremiah 15:15-19, "[Jeremiah said] O Lord, You know *and* understand; [earnestly] remember me and visit me and avenge me on my persecutors. Take me not away [from joy or from life itself] in Your long-suffering [to my enemies]; know that for Your sake I suffer *and* bear reproach. Your words were found, and I ate them; and Your words were to me a joy and the rejoicing of my heart, for I am called by Your name, O Lord God of hosts. I sat not in the assembly of those who make merry, nor did I rejoice; I sat alone because Your [powerful] hand was upon me, for You had filled me with indignation. Why is my pain perpetual and my wound incurable, refusing to be

> *"You can't use your family to judge your assignment, and you can't use your feelings to judge your assignment."*

healed? Will you indeed be to me like a deceitful brook, (I can't count on you, Lord) like waters that fail *and* are uncertain? [19] Therefore thus says the Lord [to Jeremiah]: If you return [and give up this mistaken tone of distrust and despair], then I will give you again a settled place of quiet *and* safety, and you will be My minister..." (AMP).

Though the Lord tolerated Jeremiah's grumbling, *He did not release Jeremiah from his assignment.*

How many people can you think of who gave up an assignment because they "weren't feeling it?" That's not the Kingdom way. Just like you can't use your family to judge your assignment, you can't use your feelings to reconcile your assignment. At times you might be unhappy in your assignment, but just because you might not have the joy you are anticipating in it, doesn't mean that God hasn't called you to it.

You say, "Well sir, the Lord wants me to be happy." Where do you read that? The Lord does want you to be happy, but not at the expense of being holy. Happiness is your choice, based on how you process and respond to circumstances. To be holy is to set your own agenda aside, give up your right to do your own thing and follow the way of Christ. Sometimes, you won't be happy and being holy may press you out of your comfort zone. But, if you are going to sincerely walk in your assignment and operate in the marketplace mentality, you've got to quickly adjust your attitude and become comfortable being uncomfortable.

> *"To operate in your marketplace mentality, you've got to quickly become comfortable being uncomfortable."*

God has given each believer assignments based on His specific and strategic purpose for our lives. Don't be overwhelmed by this. Embrace it and accept your task(s) with an appreciative attitude. Although you may feel inept and downright clumsy on your mountain(s) at times, know that, "...he who began a good work in you will carry it on to completion until the day of Christ Jesus." (Phil. 1:6) God is faithful; what He begins, He finishes, He polishes and He perfects.

Chapter Four

Renewing Your MIND – The Mission is HIS

From the teachings of scripture, let's clarify the word "assignment." The pre-assigned purpose or lot of an individual given by God for the intention of expanding and advancing the Kingdom—this is what a Biblical worldview of assignment means.

All assignments fall into one of two categories. There are universal assignments and there are unique assignments. Universal assignments are those things which God expects all believers to fulfill. Unique assignments are those things that correspond with the special grace that God has put on your life. There are some things that only you can do according to the grace that God has placed on your life.

Knowing your assignment releases a level of confidence in your life. In addition to releasing a certain level of confidence, knowing your assignment will also free you from expending exorbitant amounts of time on things you are not graced to do.

> *"It is righteous to say no to offers and opportunities that are not in sync with your abilities."*

When you know your purpose, when you know your charge, when you know what your assignment in the marketplace is, frustration concerning your identity will be all but eliminated. The grace God has placed on your life is the cornerstone of your success.

Some become frustrated simply by knowing that they should be doing something, but not knowing exactly what it is that they should be doing. Knowing your assignment will eliminate the frustration associated with the uncertainty of knowing whether or not you are in the place of God.

Not only will knowing your assignment eliminate frustration, knowing your assignment will also eliminate the foolishness of struggling with mismatched opportunities. It's okay to say no to offers and opportunities that are not in sync with your abilities.

Knowing your assignment will also release you from the fatigue of life. So many times, we find ourselves worn out from trying to be something that God has not called us to be. Please understand that whatever God has called you to do, he has given you a grace of ease that accompanies what He has called you to do. If you find yourself struggling to be effective in something, one of two possibilities exists: Satan is trying to sabotage your assignment or you're working in an area that God has not given you grace for. What God has called us to, he anoints us for. We will expand on this thought in Chapter Five.

To illustrate our point now, let's look at Acts 8:14-22. The Bible states in verses 14-17:

> "When the apostles in Jerusalem heard that Samaria had accepted the word of God, they sent Peter and John to Samaria. When they arrived, they prayed for the new believers there that they might receive the Holy Spirit, because the Holy Spirit had not yet come on any of them; they had simply been baptized in the name of the Lord

Jesus. Then Peter and John placed their hands on them, and they received the Holy Spirit."

This passage of scripture recounts Peter and John working within their apostolic assignment. In short, they were teachers of the gospel of Christ. We know the Lord called them to do this work because of how effective they were in leading others to not only accept Christ, but also because of the accompanying power of the Holy Spirit.

Just like in the marketplace today, there was someone who wanted what Peter and John had, even though it was not his assignment or in sync with the grace on his life. Simon the sorcerer desired a gift that was not his to have.

Still in Acts 8, verses 18-22 read:

"When Simon saw that the Spirit was given at the laying on of the apostles' hands, he offered them money and said, 'Give me also this ability so that everyone on whom I lay my hands may receive the Holy Spirit.' Peter answered: 'May your money perish with you, because you thought you could buy the gift of God with money! You have no part or share in this ministry, because your heart is not right before God. Repent of this wickedness and pray to the Lord in the hope that he may forgive you for having such a thought in your heart.'"

Rather than seeking out what God was assigning him to do, Simon coveted the gifts of Peter and John. It was not that Simon himself did not believe. He did, and he was baptized (see Acts 8:13). The fact that Simon is a believer means that God had an assignment specifically for him. However, Simon endeavors to mimic the power of the Holy Spirit as evidenced in the disciples out of impure motives. He perceived that God's assignment for Peter and John was more important than the assignment God had for him. So, instead of pursuing God for himself, Simon sought to buy what he saw. It is important to note from the scriptures that this act nearly cost Simon his life. You cannot conjure up a grace that God has not given you; on the other hand you cannot deny the grace God has given you, either. It is His work chosen to give you and I the opportunity to be involved.

How is the Kingdom of God going to be advanced if we don't see the Kingdom as more than a church? Come on, let's talk about this. How is the Kingdom going to advance if everyone is just singing in the choir? Remember, God has to scatter believers throughout the marketplace so His agenda can be advanced. We need people of influence on every mountain that can make things happen. We need people in finance that can make some things happen. We need people in education, in media, in government, in arts and entertainment, etc. that can use their influence, resources and abilities to represent God's agenda and advance the Kingdom.

> *"You cannot conjure up a grace that God has not given you; on the other hand you cannot deny the grace God has given you, either."*

We must begin to think beyond Sunday morning. Remember, it's all for the Kingdom, every mountain must be dominated by believers. We are not here to take sides, we are here to take over!

The shift in our mentality is what gives birth to the collaboration that will bring these things to bear. Though our assignment may be individual, our goal is corporate—further the gospel and advance the joy, peace, mercy and justice of the society of God.

Core belief #2–<u>Every believer has the raw material required to make an impact for the Kingdom</u>. The Lord gives gifts and assignments as a matter of His prerogative and plan for our life.

Look at the Word of God to Jeremiah, a prophet to the nations. Jeremiah 1, let's look at verse 5:

Before I formed you in the womb I knew [and] approved of you [as My chosen instrument], and before you were born I separated *and* set you apart, consecrating you; [and] I appointed you as a prophet to the nations. (AMP)

Say this aloud, "The Lord is the architect of my assignment. I don't get to determine my own assignment, that's God's business. I don't get to say what I'm going to do. Under the Lordship of Jesus Christ, I surrender my will to him."

Look at what the Lord says: "Before *I* formed you in the womb." In other words, before your daddy's sperm hit your mama's egg God purposed your life. Of all the little sperm that struggled and didn't make it, yours made it. You may have been a surprise, but you were not an accident. God had already written a plan concerning you. The choice was His that you would come forth with purpose.

I'm going to make a very bold declaration here. Please know that I mean NO insensitivity whatsoever; however concerning you, there could have been no miscarriage, because God had already written a plan. There could have been no abortion, because God had already written a plan. Even if you were born early, you had to come to full term, because God had already written a plan. As a matter of fact, your mama and daddy may not be able to tolerate each other today, but it wasn't about them. God used their passion and He used their sexual urges to accomplish something much bigger than them. Your parent's relationship may not have even lasted, but God still had a plan for your life. God said, "I need you in the earth, I need you to help advance the Kingdom."

God has written a plan for your life that only you can fulfill. It's so much better and more productive for you to work your unique God-given assignment. Remember Simon? Why attempt do what someone else is called to do, when what God has designed for you has so much more personal benefit!

One of the main reasons that we find ourselves envying or wanting another person's assignment and the grace that accompanies it is low self-esteem. For everyone reading this book, I come against every demon of low self-esteem. I curse it right now. I come against every demon that has tried to tell you you're not good enough or "you're too this," or "you're too that." No, you have all the raw material you need to excel on your mountain(s). Simply dig in and dig it out. I don't care how tall you are, how short you are, how thin you are, how wide you are, where you've come from or where you've been, you are ontologically correct – just right by God's design.

> *"God has not changed His mind about your worth and value to Him."*

Your assignment is unavoidable. Though you may run, eventually you will run right back into your assignment. Don't believe me? Just ask Jonah.

God has not changed His mind about you or your future. Neither has He changed His mind about your worth and value to Him and His Kingdom. Even with all your challenges and mistakes, God has not changed his mind.

I know there is somebody who is reading this book who has slipped along the way, and has fallen and done some things they wish they could take back. But I've come to tell you that God has not changed His mind. In His omniscience, He knew every mistake you would ever make before you would make it and He still wrote out a powerful plan for your life. Although you are not perfect, His plan concerning you is a perfect fit for you.

The Lord says in Jeremiah 1, "Before I formed you in your mother's womb and before you were born, I approved you." Did you catch that? You don't need anybody's validation. God said, "I approved you and I set you apart." God said to Jeremiah, "I ordained you to be a prophet." And then in Jeremiah 29:11, God says, "For I know the thoughts *and* plans that

I have for you, says the Lord, thoughts *and* plans for welfare *and* peace and not for evil, to give you hope in your final outcome" (AMP).

This is revelation and information. The Holy Spirit is allowing us to take a trip into the heart and mind of God concerning God's purpose over humanity. No matter what our assignment, we must trust God with not only the plan for our lives, but also with the process He uses to produce the outcome that He desires. One by one, case by case and person by person- know this—God has never made a man or a woman whom He did not have a plan for. As long as you are here, the plan is still in force.

Chapter Five

Purposed By Design

We have established that every believer has a unique singular role in God's corporate agenda. According to 1 Timothy 2:4, Matthew 28:18 and II Peter 3:9, God's agenda is very simple. We have established that God's agenda is to **bring all of humanity into the Kingdom**. Remember, a disciple is not just a follower of another; a disciple is one that adheres to the laws, the teachings and the precepts of another. And those that subscive to the teachings of the Kingdom are known as disciples of Jesus Christ.

Dr. Tony Evans in his book, "Kingdom Man" clarifies the definition of God's agenda. "The Kingdom agenda is simply the visible demonstration of the comprehensive rule of God over every area of life."[11] Again, God's agenda is to bring all of humanity into the Kingdom.

Now, in bringing all of humanity into the Kingdom, in leaving an imperative for the church to make disciples of all mankind, in understanding that the predetermined purpose, or lot of an individual is given by God for the intention of expanding and advancing the kingdom, it is clear to us according to Jeremiah chapter 1:4-5 and in Jeremiah 29:11 that it is the Lord and the Lord alone who is the architect of our place on the mountains. God and God alone is our creator, God and God alones decides our purpose.

Ephesians 1:11-12 says:

> In Him we also were made (God's) heritage (portion) *and* we obtained an inheritance; for we had been foreordained (chosen and appointed beforehand) in accordance with [what?] His purpose, Who works out everything in [what?] agreement with the counsel *and* [what?] design of His (own) will, So that we who first hoped in Christ (who first put our confidence in Him have been [what?] destined and appointed to) live for the praise of His glory! (AMP)

God has chosen you to do His bidding.

This text makes it clear you didn't choose God, God chose you. And God chose you even before the foundation of the earth. And not only did He choose you, but everything that He has done in you and every ability that He has given you is in accordance to His own purpose, His own plan and His own agenda and goal for your life.

Ephesians 4:7-8 says, "Yet grace (God's unmerited favor) was given to each of us individually [not indiscriminately, but in different ways] in proportion to the measure of Christ's [rich and bounteous] gift" (AMP).

This text tells us there is a grace that God has given us for salvation, and there is a grace that God has given us for our individual purpose and gifts. God is so meticulous that He has individually placed things inside of you and I that He intends to work in accordance with His purpose. This may be in Religion, Arts and Entertainment, Education, Family, Media, Government or Finance. The key is to not deny the significance of where and how God is using you. There is a grace for salvation, but then there is a grace to be who God has made you to be.

Consider Tyler Perry. Perry is a professed disciple of Jesus Christ. He uses his grace in Arts and Entertainment to minister healing, peace, restoration and salvation in his movies and stage plays. While humorous, seldom will you see the promotion of Christ in the form of song or dialogue, however every work illustrates Godly principles this is a prime example of embracing a marketplace mentality within the assignment that God has given us.

You and I have to be okay with being who God has called us to be and walk in the grace that God has given us to do His bidding.

Let's look at another text, I Corinthians 12:27: "Now you [collectively] are Christ's body and [individually] you are members of it" (AMP). Remember you have a singular role in God's corporate agenda. I Corinthians 12:27 affirms this revelation; Paul says collectively and corporately every believer is a part of Christ's body. Yet not only are you corporately a part of Christ's body, individually you are a member of it. This means you fulfill a necessary purpose in the body of Christ.

> "God is so meticulous that He has individually placed things inside of you and I that He intends to work in accordance with His purpose."

"Each part severally *and* distinct [each with his own place and function]. So God has appointed some in the church [for His own use]: first apostles (special messengers); second prophets (inspired preachers and expounders); third teachers; then wonder-workers; then those with ability to heal the sick; helpers; administrators; [speakers in] different (unknown) tongues." (I Corinthians 12:27b-28, AMP)

Your health would be a mess if your lungs decided, "I want to be the heart." Your body would be disproportionate if your hands decided they wanted to be your ears or if your shoulders decided they wanted to be your knees. Your pinkie toe usually doesn't get much interest and gets very little polish. You don't think very highly of it. But without your pinkie toe, your entire balance and equilibrium would be thrown off.

Most people give a lot of attention to their face, yet you can walk without your face. However, it's difficult for you to walk the way that you need to walk comfortably without something as small as your pinkie toe.

Imagine if your pinkie toe had low self-esteem or was unclear about its purpose and it said, "I'm sick and tired of the big toe getting all the attention. I don't know why the big toe gets all the love. Every time we go for a pedicure, those folk who work on our feet they spend more time on the big toe and they just run right over me. As a matter of fact, there are some days you only give the big toe a design and forget about the rest of us. And the more you get down to me, the less love you give."

You may not think much of it right now, but if it or any other part of your body did not do what it needed to do your entire body would be affected by it. It's the same way with your purpose.

What's the point, you may ask? When you don't do what God has called you to do, no matter how insignificant you may think it is, the effectiveness of the Kingdom is compromised. You are important, you are significant and the fulfillment of your assignment is necessary and required for the dominating influence of the Kingdom.

Everybody has a spiritual gift and with that gift comes your marketplace assignment. Remember, all gifts and all assignments are for the Kingdom, but all gifts and all assignments are not an episcopal assignment in the church.

Core belief #3—<u>The Lord strategically positions believers to fulfill their marketplace assignments</u>—He is the one who makes arrangements for our assignments.

Let's go to Jeremiah 1, and let's look at verse 8.

> "Be not afraid of them [their faces], for I am with you to deliver you," says the Lord. Then the Lord put forth His hand and touched my mouth. And the Lord said to me,

"Behold, I have put My words in your mouth. See, I have this day appointed you to the oversight of the nations and of the kingdoms to root out and pull down, to destroy and to overthrow, to build and to plant." Moreover, the word of the Lord came to me, saying, "Jeremiah, what do you see?" And I said, "I see a branch *or* shoot of an almond tree [the emblem of alertness and activity, blossoming in late winter]." Then said the Lord to me, "You have seen well, for I am alert *and* active watching over My word to perform it." (AMP)

Essentially, this is what the LORD is saying: "You have seen well. For I am alert, I'm active. I know what I spoke over your life Jeremiah. I know what I called you to do, Jeremiah. I know the plans that I have for you, Jeremiah. I know what I have promised you, I know what I told you I was going to do for you, what I told you I was going to bring to pass on your behalf. I'm watching over that Word, The Word of prophecy that I've just spoken over you, Jeremiah, and I am watching over this Word of confirmation, Jeremiah. I'm not saying that it's going to be easy, but I'm watching over what I've spoken over you. And I'm going to make sure it comes to pass. I'm watching over my Word to perform it." Just as the Lord spoke these things to Jeremiah, He is speaking the same thing to us today.

Look at verse 12. "Then said the Lord to me..." Pause right there. Now this is after God has told Jeremiah, "I have anointed you; I have appointed you to be my prophet. Before you even entered into your mother's womb, I ordained you and anointed you as a prophet unto myself. Jeremiah's response is, "Lord, I'm too young." And the Lord says, "Don't say I'm too young. I'm with you. I'm going to do in you what only I can do in you." In verse 12, God says, "Jeremiah, what do you see?" Jeremiah says, "I see an almond tree." The Lord says, "You see well..."

The thing that distinguished the almond tree is that the almond tree would bear fruit when other trees went into a season of dormancy. The almond tree is the tree that would blossom in the winter when everything else was dead. It was known as the alert tree. It was known as the vigilant tree. In Hebrew, it's "shaqed." It was known as the watching tree. It's always there. And that's what God says to Jeremiah. Look at Jeremiah 1:12.

> Then said the Lord to me, "You have seen well, for I am alert *and* active, (I am) watching over My word to perform it. I know what I've spoken over your life, Jeremiah and I am watching over what I have spoken over your life to see to it that it comes to pass."

You see, when the Lord speaks something over your life, it ceases to be about you. From that moment on it's about Him, and His name, and His character and His integrity. If God doesn't do it, then that makes God a liar. And God has never lied to anybody in history and you won't be the first person in history that He breaks His record for.

How then do we reconcile this reality that God makes arrangements for our assignment(s) and the reality that we are stewards over our assignment? It's not hard really because the truth is there are some things that only God can pull off. God does not expect you to do what only God can do. He does what only He can do and we are responsible for stewarding and maximizing the fruit of His work in our lives. Only God can impregnate a virgin and she still be a virgin. God arranged a virgin conception and a virgin birth, and yet Mary still had to take Jesus to the temple.

Allow your mind to accept this truth—what looks like a setback may be God making an arrangement to set you up to fulfill your assignment. It may not happen the way you thought it was going to happen, it may not even happen with the people you thought it was going to happen with, but if God said it that settles it, it's going to happen.

There are two reasons why the Lord makes arrangements for our assignment. . Number one, The Lord makes arrangements for our assignment(s) for His glory. Matthew 5:16 says: "Let your light so shine before men that they may see your moral excellence and your praiseworthy, noble, *and* good deeds *and* recognize *and* honor *and* praise *and* glorify your Father Who is in heaven"(AMP).

If you still have a deep need to be recognized, your mentality is under-developed and needs greater maintenance. If you have a need to be under the spotlight, to have your name called, to have your name listed, then you're not ready for high elevation, or to work in the places God wants you to work in to bring transformation for His glory.

When you try to get in the way of God's glory then you become ineffective and end up relying on your own grace. However, when you submit your grace to the Giver of the grace for His glory is when greater graces are released. When you want glory for yourself, when you're trying to make a name for yourself apart from the purpose of God – you might receive some glory, but it will be the lesser glory of your design and not the greater Glory of God for the Kingdom. Don't miss a blessing trying to make a blessing.

The second reason the Lord positions believers and creates opportunities for His disciples to work in their grace is for the growth of the Kingdom.

> Luke 13:18-20: "This led Him to say, What is the kingdom of God like? And to what shall I compare it? [19]It is like a grain of mustard seed, which a man took and planted in his own garden; and it grew and became a tree, and the wild birds found shelter *and* roosted *and* nested in its

branches.[20] And again He said, To what shall I liken the kingdom of God? It is like leaven which a woman took and hid in three measures of wheat flour *or* meal until it was all leavened (fermented)." (AMP)

There is such a synergy concerning the Kingdom that sometimes the Lord positions you to be a conduit for the assignment of another. This is why it is important that we maximize our connections. A great example of a mind renewed toward maximizing connections—doing something natural so that something spiritual can take place and the usage of raw materials—is found in the Old Testament miracle in 2 Kings 4. The woman of this story is a widow who is so devastated by her economic condition that she only imagined a future of servitude for her to settle the family debt. The law stated that a person had to offer themselves or their children as slaves to work off debt that could not be paid.

Notice that Elijah's question to her was, "What do you have in your house?" She replies that she has a little oil and a couple of jars. This woman had no idea when she woke up that morning that not only would she be debt free but that she would start a successful business. Her mind was bent toward defeat and devastation.

We are not surprised by the miracle of the oil becoming a surplus. The Bible is a book of miracles. *The wisdom of Elijah is perhaps the most shocking aspect of the text.* You would surmise that as a man of God He would have told her to "pray" or "fast" or "make a faith confession" or "praise the Lord." Elijah tells her to do none of the above. What does he do? He activates a business plan in the mind of the woman.

Certainly prayer, fasting, praise or making a faith confession would have turned her situation around. However, what she needed most was a renewed mind concerning the usage of her raw material, the maximizing of her connections and the law of the natural to set a stage for the supernatural change she needed. God had the miracle for her all along, however the manifestation came through the renewal of her mind. Elijah tells her to go to her neighbors and borrow jars. He even qualified it by telling her to borrow as many jars as she could get her hands on.

The Lord had strategically positioned Elijah in the life of the widow to bring her into a marketplace mentality and challenge her crippling mentality. History does not tell us anymore about this woman outside of the first few verses recorded concerning her in this text. However, we can surmise that this woman went on to not only have a successful business in her generation; she also established a new pattern of thinking for her sons. Can you imagine not only the wealth but the influence she garnered in her community?

> *"When you try to get in the way of God's glory, then you become ineffective. However, when you submit your grace to the Giver of the grace for His glory is when greater graces are released."*

An example of a well-intentioned but crippling mentality is found in the familiar proverb about fish. Perhaps you have heard it:

"Give a man a fish and he eats for a day, teach a man to fish and you feed him for a lifetime."

The marketplace mentality doesn't want to only eat fish or go fishing. The marketplace mentality wants to OWN the lake where others come to fish.

Wherever God has planted you, it is so that you can be a part of the growth and expansion of the Kingdom. Please remember that the Kingdom is not just the church. It is the rule, authority, dominion and reign of God. This includes dominion over Education, Arts and Entertainment, Family, Government, Religion, Media and Finance.

God says the Kingdom of God is like a mustard seed that is planted in a field, but it doesn't stay a seed. It grows and becomes strong and has so much strength to it that birds can build their nests in it. That's what God wants for the Kingdom. He wants the Kingdom to grow. God says the Kingdom of God is like a mustard seed that is planted in a field, but it doesn't stay a seed. It grows and becomes so strong, and has so much strength to it that birds can build their nests in it. But He also wants the Kingdom to be strong and stable, something that the world can lean and build upon.

The Lord is consistently seeing to it that the grace that He has placed on your life is pressed out to the furthest edges of the world for His glory and for the growth of the Kingdom. This is why I said to you in the last chapter, "It's all for the Kingdom, but it's not all in the church." See, if every gift was just in the church the Kingdom couldn't possibly be positioned to expand. God needs Kingdom-minded attorneys, and Kingdom-minded Financiers, and He needs Kingdom-minded teachers and He needs Kingdom-minded architects and Kingdom-minded politicians, He needs Kingdom-minded contractors and the list goes on.

It's all for the glory of God and the growth and expansion of the Kingdom.

Chapter Six

You Are Anointed!

David is one of the most familiar personalities in Scripture. His life has been the source of theological fascination for centuries. The way in which David is selected for the throne of Israel is an expression of the reality of a sovereign God. I Samuel 16:13 reads:

"Then Samuel took the horn of oil and anointed David in the midst of his brothers; and the Spirit of the Lord came mightily upon David from that day forward. And Samuel arose and went to Ramah" (AMP).

Now, I'm about to tell you something, but I want you to sit down—this is heavy. The Lord has anointed you for your purpose.

Core belief #4 – <u>You are anointed.</u>

Now listen to this, please pay attention to this. We have such an ungodly, soft-secular understanding of the anointing. The reason I say this is because we have "celebritized" and compartmentalized the anointing and we have made the anointing more about something we see than about something we are. You are anointed, and you are not anointed because of the version of the Bible that you carry. You are not anointed because of the spiritual gift you have. You are not even anointed because of your denomination or your preacher.

What does it really mean to be anointed? We need to settle this once and for all. Here exists an awesome opportunity For us to allow our mind to be renewed concerning the anointing.

Let's look at 1 Samuel 16, again, verse 13. It says, "Then Samuel took the horn of oil and anointed David in the midst of his brothers..."

Now this lets me know right here that to be anointed simply means to receive the enablement of God. Again, anointed means "God has made you able." The Bible says that after Samuel poured the oil on David that the Spirit of the Lord came upon him from that day forward. Now earlier in the text, Samuel poured oil on David's seven brothers and guess what happened? <u>Nothing</u>. Having oil put on you is NOT what makes you anointed. If the Spirit of God does not accompany the oil, you're just greasy.

> *"To be anointed simply means to receive the enablement of God."*

Whatever the Lord's assignment(s) is/are for your life, the anointing to get it done is within you. The Lord has made you able. Please do not dismiss the power of the supernatural in your life.

Seldom do we consider that someone can be anointed outside of the Mountain of Religion (i.e. church). However, being that the Kingdom is not just the church then we must not dismiss the revelation that believers in Government are no less anointed than the Missionary in Africa. Both are a critical part of the expansion of the Kingdom. Both the missionary in Africa and the prime minister have been made able by God, both are anointed for their assignments.

This is the <u>*same level*</u> of anointing Jesus possessed. Think about it, you and Jesus have been made able by the exact same God!

The Lord anoints for and with purpose, which means whatever mountain God has called you to dominate, He has also enabled you to do so. Listen to the words of our Lord in Luke 4:18:

"The Spirit of the Lord [is] upon Me, because He has anointed Me [the Anointed One, the Messiah] (He has made me able) to preach the good news (the Gospel) to the poor; He has sent Me to announce release to the captives and recovery of sight to the blind, to send forth as delivered those who are oppressed [who are downtrodden, bruised, crushed, and broken down by calamity]" (AMP).

In other words, Jesus says, "God has made me able to preach the good news. God has given me the strength, skill and stamina that is required, along with the support and the substance that is required to complete every mission He assigned." My friend, Dr. Calvin McFadden says, "The Lord does not audition people. He anoints people." Whatever God has called you to do, He isn't trying you out for it. He just makes you able.

> *"As needs arise, anointing arises. As needs shift, anointing shifts."*

Some people try to audition for things that are not in God's plan for them and it never works. When God hasn't chosen to gift you with something, you don't have it, there's nothing you can do to get it. Yet when God has gifted and anointed you in any area you have it and room is always made for you to use it. Pause and read that paragraph again.

This raises the issue of necessity. Please be sensitive to understand that you are only anointed out of necessity. God makes you able only where there is a need, because the Lord doesn't waste or squander the precious resource of His anointing. You are anointed for something because there is a need for it. As needs arise, anointing arises. As needs shift, anointing shifts.

When Jesus first came to earth, He was anointed to preach the gospel of the Kingdom (Matt. 24:14). There was a need for it. But when He comes back, there's going to be a shift in His anointing. He's not coming back to preach the gospel of the Kingdom. No, He's not coming back to work miracles. He's worked His miracles while He was here the first time and any other miracles that show up in the earth are going to show up through you and I who embody His presence. When He comes back, it will be fulfill eschatological prophecy. There will have been a shift in His anointing.

One of the challenges that we have is to make sure you don't get stuck in a former anointing or an anointing for an age that has passed; you've got to be sensitive to adjustments in your anointing. If you are able to develop this discernment, it will ensure that you are never useless or washed up. You're always evolving and becoming whatever it is that God requires you to be.

In the secular world, they call it a second career. But really, it's not a second career; it's a shift in your anointing. In one season of your life, God may purpose you for one thing, but there may be another need that arises that God purposes you for in another season. You might have started off operating in the Mountain of Finance, now you may be in the Mountain of Education.

> "Our instincts, interests and natural abilities are generally signposts to our Kingdom contribution."

Accepting this truth will deliver you from feeling like you are indecisive and overly busy but without specific purpose. People may mock you and say, "You're old, you're a grandmother or you're a grandfather. Why in the world would you be going back to school at your age?" Remember these comments are made out of their limited revelation. Tell them, "I discern a shift in my anointing. I'm just trying to be used of God, and I'll go until I'm ninety if God enables me to do so. Because I want to be whatever God burdens me to be according to the needs that exist." This in no way means that you are cut off from your former ability. It just means that you are open to new graces for your life.

Let's take a look at II Timothy 4. Remember we noted that the first time the Lord Jesus came to earth He was anointed to preach the gospel of the Kingdom and to work miracles. But when He comes back, we'll see something different. II Timothy 4:1:

> "I charge [you] in the presence of God and of Christ Jesus, Who is to judge the living and the dead, and by (in the light of) His coming and His kingdom."

Paul lets us know that Jesus Christ is coming back to judge. The first time He came He came to save. See the shift? Next time He's coming to judge.

We see the same thing happen in David's life. David starts off keeping sheep. Later he experiences a shift in his anointing. And he goes from keeping sheep to ruling the nation.

An interesting observation about the anointing and our abilities is that oftentimes it is not until the revelation of God comes that we recognize the close tie of our natural instincts, interests and abilities as our area of anointing. Our instincts, interests and natural abilities are generally signposts to our Kingdom contribution.

As a child, I was a huge fan of the theater. I was often the lead character in school plays. To this day, I have dozens of 1st place awards from speech contests. Additionally, I was the first student elected by my peers to serve on the Dayton Board of Education. It was almost as if in every setting I ascended to leadership. These same instincts, interests and natural abilities have been very valuable to me in ministry. The Holy Spirit simply arrested them for the Mountain of Religion.

Whatever you were able to do in the world, it's often just a matter of surrendering it to God. Also be aware of this—the devil will always attempt to pervert your ability.

Remember Rahab? Rahab shows up in Joshua 2. Rahab had a tremendous ability; she just hadn't surrendered it for righteousness. For those who may not be familiar with Rahab's story, she was a whore and she is related to our Savior Jesus Christ. One of Jesus' great grandmothers was a whore. Not only was she a whore, but She was a lying whore. To be a good whore, she must have had the spirit of hospitality. She knew how to entertain men, she knew how to make them feel comfortable and she knew how to keep their secrets. So when two spies came along, she was presented with the opportunity for her to apply her hospitality ability for the Kingdom.

Our natural abilities must be surrendered to God for the prosperity of the Kingdom. The same God that provides us with our abilities is the same God who has given us free will. It is indeed the exercise of the enemy to seduce us to use our abilities in unrighteous ways. Using our abilities in any way that is opposite of the Kingdom way is unrighteousness.

Consider this example: I grew up in a public housing complex in Dayton, Oh. In the late 80's it was one of the most drug infested communities in the city. It was very common for young men to forgo school in lieu of selling drugs. Drug trafficking was a major enterprise in my neighborhood. When you consider the skill sets required for such an enterprise, they parallel the skill sets needed to operate a successful legitimate business.

Marketing, supply and demand, research and development, human resources, product placement and customer service are just some of the skills required for a successful business. Now imagine a person with those skills applied for the increase of the Kingdom.

Let's look at the men Jesus chose as his disciples. All were ordinary men. Matthew was a tax collector; Judas was an accountant; Simon was a politician. Andrew and Peter, who were brothers, were fishermen just like their father and their grandfather. James and John (the sons of Zebedee) were also fishermen. It's important to note that before their encounter with Jesus, none of them were devoutly religious or had religious titles. But Perhaps Jesus chose them in part because of the potential of their natural abilities to make disciples of others. What they were lacking in their natural abilities was a Kingdom worldview and a greater awareness of their potential.

Listen to the words of Jesus, "Come with me and I will make you fishers of men" (Matt. 4:19). They already had the ability to fish for fish; He said, "I'm going to make you fishers of men." As fishers of men, they would have to use the right bait. They would have to know when the fish are most receptive, where the fish were and they would have to employ patience. Similar skills, different application.

Remember Paul the Apostle? God taught him how to redirect his passion and his abilities. As Saul, he was known as a great intellectual thinker. He studied logic with the leading philosophical scholars, he knew how to respect detail, how to analyze, how to visualize the end result and he was fluent in several languages. As Saul, he vigorously persecuted the church and even participated in the stoning of Stephen, one of the early disciples. Acts 8:3 tells us he went so far as to go door to door, interrogating people about their belief in Jesus and punishing them on the spot. Saul became legendary in his persecution of the church. There was no question of Saul's ability; it was that he had not surrendered it to the Kingdom.

We know according to Acts 9 that Saul had a transforming experience while on his way to Damascus. After that experience Paul then, with the same intensity and vigor that he utilized to persecute the church began to preach, make disciples and became an aggressive defender of salvation for the Gentiles. Paul's influence was so vast that most of the New Testament was written by him.

> *"How you apply your ability and skills is critical."*

This is the point, how you apply your abilities and skills is critical. Many positive and negative activities in life require the same or similar skills. Whether it is indeed positive or negative largely comes down to the application of the skills. Remember, Satan desires to trick you into using your ability for carnal reasons. Continually realign yourself with God and you will fulfill the purpose that He has anointed you for.

Chapter Seven

The No Compromise Zone

We've identified several critical core beliefs. Let's quickly recap them. <u>Core Belief #1—The Kingdom is more than what we experience within our places of worship</u>. Everyone has a God-given assignment. We know that assignment is the pre-determined purpose, or lot of an individual given by God for the intention of expanding the Kingdom.

<u>Core belief #2—Every believer has the raw materials required for making an impact for the Kingdom</u>. Every believer has a unique, singular role in God's corporate agenda. And every believer has been given specific graces in view of God's intention for their life. God's corporate agenda is to bring everyone, all of humanity into the Kingdom under His rule, under His Lordship, and under His authority.

We've also said that you and I don't have a say in determining the Lord's agenda for our life. Our voice is limited to the extent that we are able to exercise our free will. This takes us to <u>core belief #3—The Lord strategically positions believers to fulfill their assignment in the marketplace.</u> The Lord is the architect of our assignment; He places believers on the mountains. God tells Jeremiah, "Before I formed you in your mother's womb, I anointed you, I ordained you, I set you forth as a prophet to the nations."

There are two reasons for our assignments. The Lord designs our assignment for His glory and the growth of the Kingdom. Let's start with glory. God is glorified by putting visibility on the invisibility of His power. God is a healer—*healer* is invisible. But when God heals *you*, healing becomes visible. He puts visibility on the invisibility of His power and we rejoice! We can talk all day long about God being a provider, but your provision is invisible until it manifests. The manifestation is the glory. It is as believers operate in excellence on the mountains of their assignment(s) that God is glorified.

Secondly, God designs our assignment for the growth and the expansion of the Kingdom. In the Word, Jesus gives us the parable of a man who had sown a mustard seed in the field. That seed grows into a tree. It is so vital a tree that birds come along and rest in the tree, build their nest in the tree and nurse their young in the tree. The Kingdom was never intended to be contained or covert. Glory and growth – this is the mind of God concerning your assignment.

<u>Core belief #4—God anoints us for our assignment in the Kingdom.</u>

To be anointed is so much more than someone applying oil to your head. To be anointed means the Lord has made you able. You're not anointed because of anything mystical that has happened to you, you are anointed because the Lord has given you certain abilities. When you identify your ability, you will likely identify your anointing. Satan intends to pervert your abilities so that you can miss your anointing. Your anointing is often encased in your natural ability.

We looked at Rahab; for years she misapplied her ability. The Bible says she was a woman of ill repute. She had the spirit of hospitality; she knew how to make men feel welcome. She knew how to win men's confidence. But it is when she met Joshua and Caleb that she recognized an opportunity to redirect her abilities. When you search the genealogy of Jesus Christ, Rahab shows up as one of the grandmothers of our Lord.

Jesus didn't come from the 'right' side of the tracks; he came from a family just like yours and mine. Skeletons in the closet, bodies buried in the backyard, things you'd rather not talk about, etc. Jesus was born in a family who was very familiar with common human experiences.

While the Lord is the architect of our assignments, we are the stewards of our assignments. God has a major plan in mind for you – point to yourself and say, for me, for me." How you exercise your authority will influence how you flourish in your assignment.

Think about this–The Lord didn't show up on the side of your bed, wake you up, put your socks on you, brush your teeth, wash your face, and tell you put this on or that on this morning. The Lord didn't sit in the driver's seat of your car, tell you to get in the back seat of your car seat, strap you in your seatbelt, etc. No, there are certain details that the Lord simply leaves to us–things such as how we manage our time, how we nurture our relationships, etc. The level at which we steward our assignment will determine our effectiveness and our harvest. This why Paul writes in 1 Corinthians 15:10, "But by the grace of God I am what I am, and his grace to me was not without effect. No, I worked harder than all of them—yet not I, but the grace of God that was with me."

I Corinthians 4 is another passage that upholds this profound truth. I Corinthians 4:1-2, "So then, let us [apostles] be looked upon as ministering servants of Christ and stewards (trustees) of the mysteries (the secret purposes) of God. Moreover, it is [essentially] required of stewards that a man should be found faithful [proving himself worthy of trust]."

Paul emphasizes the fact that as an apostle it was incumbent upon him to be devout, diligent and disciplined. Paul recognized the Lord had required him to be a good steward over his calling.

The enemy is ever on a mission to compromise our authority and seduce us into a less than diligent steward mentality. Bishop I.V. Hilliard once noted several ways the believer's authority can be compromised.

Sometimes our authority is compromised because of social conditioning. There's an example of that in Judges 21:25, "In those days there was no king in Israel. There was no rule, no authority and no government. Look at the results of the absence of responsible authority or government. "Every man did what was right in his own eyes." Our authority can be compromised by social conditioning or based upon the social norms of our environment. Compromised authority is the impairing of judgments or the inability to focus on priorities due to circumstances either invented or inherited.

This is why the Word of God tells us that bad company can corrupt or pollute good manners (1 Cor. 15:33). Environment does matter. If you are going to be a good steward, you must not be cavalier about the prudence required to cultivate life giving social circles. Our authority is only beneficial to the extent that we exercise it in agreement with God's Word. Because sometimes we can become unsuspecting products of our environment, we must be careful to consider that there may be worldviews we subscribe to that are contrary to the mind of God.

The effectiveness of our assignment can be compromised through social conditioning. Another example of this can be found in Proverbs 29:18. "Where there is no vision [no redemptive revelation of God], the people perish; (the people cast off restraint) but he who keeps the law [of God, which includes that of man]—blessed (happy, fortunate, and enviable) is he." (AMP). If there is an environment where God's Word is not the standard, the effectiveness of our assignment can be compromised.

I was listening to the commentary about the tragic school shooting in Newton, Connecticut in December 2012. Bill Schaeffer from CNN made an interesting statement. Schaeffer said, "I'm wondering if this is America's new normal." From there he started running down the line of tragedies that America experienced over the span of one decade. From Aurora to Columbine to Paducah, Kentucky. When God's Word is not the standard, normal is always shifting which leads to new social conditioning. All of these are prime examples of how our authority is compromised because of the influence of social conditioning.

Hilliard also says our authority is sometimes compromised because of satanic confusion. The enemy rarely gets in a fight, but he's real good at starting fights. Satan works by influencing the mind and actions of others in an effort to cause confusion. I often say, "People can be used of the enemy even when they don't mean to be."

Look at I Corinthians 14:33. "For He [Who is the source of their prophesying] is not a God of confusion *and* disorder but of peace *and* order. As [is the practice] in all the churches of the saints [God's people]." (AMP)

Let us not forget, Satan is a spirit. He needs a body and somebody he can work through. Confusion is a spirit. Disorder is a spirit. And it needs a body, somebody it can work its work through. Sometimes your authority is compromised because Satan has drawn you away by a spirit of confusion. It can be in your family, in your marriage, in your house, on your job, in your church, on your row, concerning your money, concerning your body, your heart, your mind or any other area of your life. Don't let satanic confusion compromise the stewarding of your assignment.

Bishop Hilliard also says another way our authority is sometimes compromised is through sabotaging conversation. Look at Jeremiah 1:6. "Then said I, Ah, Lord God! Behold, I cannot speak, for I am only a youth. But the Lord said to me, Say not, I am only a youth." Look here, this is the same thing the Lord is saying to you. Maybe your response is not "Lord, I'm only a youth." Maybe your response is, "Lord, I'm only one person." The Lord says, "Uh-uh, don't you say I'm only one person." "But Lord, I'm too old." "Uh-uh, don't you say I'm too old."

The fact age, social status, economics, family history, etc. can all become non-factors is what makes it a God thing. God can use the finite: God can take somebody young; God can take somebody who used to be an addict; that God can take somebody that used to be a drunkard...I could go on, but I think you get the point. The fact that God can use the life of even those most unlikely and get glory out of it is a testament to His sovereignty.

The key for you and I is to confess that we can live out and up to our ability. Your behavior will ALWAYS meet the level of your words! Your thoughts determine your words, and your words determine your actions. If you think you can't, you will say you can't and then you won't! You must refuse to say you can't where God says you can. Don't say you won't where God says you will. Don't say you are not what God says you are. "..Now let the weak say I am strong" (Joel 3:10) is the way of our God. Again, God teaches us that the strength of our thinking and the extent of our behavior will ALWAYS meet the level of our confession.

If God says you can, believe you can. If God says you will, believe you will. If God says it's on you, you can't change it; it's just on you. If God says it's yours, believe it's yours. If God says He's going to do it, believe He's going to do it. You have to be sure that you don't allow your mouth to betray your assignment. The words that come out of your mouth live in your future, so choose your words wisely! You shall have what you say (Mark 11:23). Commit to only speak words that affirm the potential of your assignment.

Finally, sensual or soulish choices can compromise your authority. How you make decisions and the material that you use to make decisions will impact the quality of steward you are over your assignment. If you make decisions exclusively out of your natural understanding, you are pulling on your sensual or soulish nature. Decisions made apart from the influence of the kingdom will seldom yield lasting, good successes.

Upon the creation of Adam, the Lord relinquished His authority regarding the stewarding of earthly assignments to humanity. The Lord used His authority in creation and then He stepped back.

Genesis 1:26-30 states, "And God said let us (Father, Son and Holy Spirit) make mankind in our own image, after our likeness. And let them have complete authority over the earth." (AMP) *Complete authority.*

To understand God's mind regarding this, let's look at the book of Genesis. Notice that every time God spoke to Adam it is recorded The LORD GOD. Some etymological probing reveals The LORD GOD in the original language are the words JEHOVAH Elohim[12] which is translated as ruler and JEHOVAH Adonai[13] which is translated as master.

However, when Satan went to Eve, he didn't say, "... has it been written that the *LORD GOD* has said?" Satan stated, "...has it been written that 'God said?'". Satan de-emphasized the absolute authority of God over Adam and Eve, and as a result he was able to manipulate Eve's authority. Had Satan said 'the LORD GOD', he wouldn't have succeeded because Eve would have had an auditory reminder that she and Adam were under the absolute Lordship of JEHOVAH.

> *"The only thing that can keep you from your best is the quality of the space between your ears. Improve your thoughts and you will improve your life. "*

Although God has released complete authority to mankind over creation, God never intended for man to rule himself. The only way your authority will profit your marketplace assignment is for you exercise it in agreement with God's Word.

This revelation is critical to the formation of a marketplace mentality. The Bible alone must shape your core beliefs. This is how the influence of the Kingdom is established. How you view your personal authority must receive maintenance from the Word of God.

Core belief #5 – <u>The mind is neutral</u>. It is becomes an asset or a liability based on how we cultivate it. That is why we must have a complete understanding of how the authority God has given us as believers. This revelation is critical to a formation of a Marketplace Mentality. Because the mind is neutral, the Word and the Word alone must shape your core beliefs. How you view your personal authority must receive maintenance from the Word of God.

The one thing that keeps many believers from their best is the quality of the space between their ears. As your mind is renewed and the quality of space between our ears improves, our decisions and what we experience as a result of those decisions will improve, also.

This goal of this level of renewed thinking concerning authority is to usher believers further into submission to God and to His Word. In the Old Testament God subjugated His authority to humanity by way of Adam. In the New Testament, God subjugated His authority by way of the second Adam, who is Jesus Christ. We see this in Matthew 28:18, "Then Jesus came to them and said, "All authority in heaven and on earth has been given to me."

Now look at what Jesus did with His authority. Look at Matthew 16:19. The Lord releases authority to us over our assignment.

"I will give you the keys of the kingdom of heaven; and whatever you bind (declare to be improper and unlawful) on earth must be what is already bound in heaven; and whatever you loose (declare lawful) on earth must be what is already loosed in heaven." (AMP)

The Word of God is the believers' constitution; it is to govern every part of our life. So yes, you have authority, but you're not in control. Success, indeed good success is the readiness of mind to submit your actions to the counsel of the Word.

Look at Deuteronomy 30:15-18.

> "See, I have set before you this day life and good, and death and evil. [If you obey the commandments of the Lord your God which] I command you today, to love the

Lord your God, to walk in His ways, and to keep His commandments and His statutes and His ordinances, then you shall live and multiply, and the Lord your God will bless you in the land into which you go to possess. But if your [mind and] heart turn away and you will not hear, but are drawn away to worship other gods and serve them, I declare to you today that you shall surely perish, and you shall not live long in the land which you pass over the Jordan to enter and possess." (AMP)

We see a parallel text in the New Testament. It is recorded in Matthew 6:33, "But seek (aim at and strive after) first of all His kingdom and His righteousness (His way of doing and being right), and then all these things taken together will be given you besides." (AMP)

The influence we have over our lives is considerable; we have authority. Have you ever looked at some people and wondered how did their life get like that? They were seduced away from revelation concerning their authority and misappropriated what God had given them.

Do your faith a favor and stop trying to make everything that you see God's will. That's the easy way out and it has been a way of us not fully accepting responsibility for 'our stuff'.

If I step off the curb in front of a bus, and that bus kills me, Please don't say, "it must have been his time". No, getting killed by a bus would certainly not be the will of God. I have small children and there are so many things that I'm still believing God to bring to pass. No, I just didn't see the bus coming, something awful happened or I misused the authority God gave me.

God desires good things for us, however to attain all the benefits associated with our assignment, we must constantly align our authority with His Kingdom principles.

Jesus has given believers authority. However, the only way our authority is going to be fruitful is as we surrender it back to the Lord in agreement with His Word. Know this, that whenever you use your authority in a way that is not in agreement with the Kingdom, the Lord does not honor it. Whatever the Lord does not honor will not last.

Chapter Eight

Release Your Influence

It is undeniable that the culture of the Kingdom must be released over every influence and mountain of the world. Earlier we discussed how all assignments/responsibilities fall into one of two categories- universal and unique. Universal assignments/responsibilities are those things God expects for every one of His followers to execute. Let's consider universal assignments as the minimum that a believer should do and unique assignments to be the maximum can do. Let's test these categories against the scriptures.

Hebrews 10:25, "Not forsaking *or* neglecting to assemble together [as believers], as is the habit of some people, but admonishing (warning, urging, and encouraging) one another, and all the more faithfully as you see the day approaching."

Some pragmatic ways in which universal assignments are illustrated are through: sharing our faith with others; connecting with God and other believers; maturing and growing in the faith; serving and performing works of mercy toward our world.

God expects every believer to be connected vertically and horizontally. Our horizontal connection is with other believers, particularly through the local church. Although some see the contemporary church as ineffective and question its relevance, the church remains the only mountain for which the Lord is coming back. The Lord expects every believer to be connected to a local church.

The Lord also expects every believer to be a growing believer. This is evidenced in Luke 2:52, "And Jesus increased in wisdom (in broad and full understanding) and in stature *and* years, and in favor with God and man." (AMP)The King James Version says, "And Jesus grew..." This is what the Bible says about, Jesus the Lord of our salvation. If Jesus had to grow, and He's God in the flesh, you and I are not exempt from doing the same.

The call of God on your life requires an ever evolving, higher level of maturity. It requires a higher level of understanding. As God continues to make your assignment known to you, the quality of wisdom, understanding, and decision-making you exhibit must increase as well. Without a continual commitment to growing you will not reach your personal best.

It is important to point out the pattern and extent of the Lord's growth. Jesus did not simply grow in His spirituality, He grew intellectually as well. This is a critical observation. One of my mentors Dr. Kevin Cosby says concerning this passage of scripture, "There is a pattern of the spiritual and the practical maturity of the Lord. The same is required of you and me."

We must be as intellectually, spiritually and practically informed as possible. This includes having knowledge of the condition of our communities: rising precedents; social norms; economic threats; trends; health considerations, etc. This information is critical to recognizing opportunities in which we who are Kingdom citizens can garner more influence for the Kingdom. What better way to attain influence for the cause of Christ than to be in a position to offer solutions to a society who is grappling with these challenges?

Mark 10:44 gives us revelation on the universal burden of believers to serve: "And whoever wishes to be most important *and* first in rank among you must be slave of all. For even the Son of Man came not to have service rendered to Him, but to serve, and to give His life as a ransom for (instead of) many" (AMP).

What does this mean? Whoever wishes to truly be significant from God's perspective, whoever wishes to be great must understand that the way to greatness is by serving.

The Greek word for great is *mega*. This is interesting considering the way most Western Christians understand the word mega. We refer to a "mega church" any church that has more than 2,000 regular participants, but that's not what God calls a mega church. God doesn't measure mega by the number of people who are sitting, God measures mega by the number of people who are about the business of serving. The Lord not only counts serving as significant, He also counts it as great. What selfless thing are you doing to intentionally improve the quality of someone else's existence?

Recall the imperative concerning serving found in 1 Peter 4:10-11:

"Each of you should use whatever gift you have received to serve others, as faithful stewards of God's grace in its various forms. [11] ... If anyone serves, they should do so with the strength God provides, so that in all things God may be praised through Jesus Christ..."

Finally, our Lord expects that all believers will demonstrate acts of mercy, sharing our faith with others to meeting the needs of others through acts of practical goodness.

Jesus encapsulates the imperative to share our faith in the word, *"go"*. In Matthew 28:19, we are told to "...go then and make disciples..."(AMP); and in Luke 14:23, we are told to, "...go out into the highways and hedges and urge and constrain [them] to yield and come in...".(AMP)

Within these scriptures, we see God's heart toward Evangelism. While this is one of the most impactful offensive efforts of the church, we find that Evangelism is most effective when paired with Missions.

Matthew 25:35-36, "For I was hungry and you gave Me food, I was thirsty and you gave Me something to drink, I was a stranger and you brought Me together with yourselves *and* welcomed *and* entertained *and* lodged Me,' was naked and you clothed Me, I was sick and you visited Me with help *and* ministering care, I was in prison and you came to see Me."

Through this parable, Jesus illuminates that meeting the everyday, natural needs of others is a demonstration of our spiritual devotion to Him. Matthew 25:40 states, "...Truly I tell you, in so far as you did it for one of the least [in the estimation of men] of these My brethren, you did it for Me." (AMP) Without both Evangelism (the heart of God) and Missions (the hand of God) being demonstrated by believers the Kingdom Agenda (bringing others into relationship with Christ) is stifled.

How do we maximize our mandate from the Kingdom and release the full potential of our influence? The answer is simple and yet profound. Our mandate to advance the Kingdom is maximized and the weight of our influence is deposited in the earth when we live the width of our unique assignment.

Core belief #6 – Believers are called to do the most not the least. I have six beautiful kids and one of them is very adept at keeping me current on new nomenclature; Trinity. Every now and then when I am doing more than what she feels is reasonable or required, she will say to me "Daddy, you are doing the most." As a kid she usually means this in the most sarcastic and unnecessary way possible. However, I have learned to take it as a compliment. A marketplace mentality demands that we not skirt by or just do enough, it means that we deliberately "do the most"!

In a world where the mundane and mediocre are celebrated and rewarded it can seem entirely unnecessary to intentionally go all out and do "the most." Yet, this is what gives greater strength to the kingdom agenda and what truly validates our unique assignments. You must purpose to live the width of every available ability the Lord has graced you with. Don't live just the length of your abilities, live the width. There is so much more you and I can do for the kingdom if we would just stretch ourselves a little more and do the most.

The Lord wants to use you to impact, enhance and influence everything and everyone within your reach. Too many people die having lived a straight line. They haven't left a mark that cannot be erased; they haven't left an impact proportionate to their unique assignment; impacted anybody; they haven't enhanced their territory with the maximum impact; they have not been agents of change and restoration to the extent of their potential.

The Lord wants you and me to follow the narrow path of being governed by His way, but He does not want you to live a straight line. There is more in you! You have lives to touch and an inheritance to bring forth that you won't if you don't expand your reach. God's will is that you get beyond your comfort zone, dig in and stretch out so you can have the maximum impact for the Kingdom and a greater recompense through your assignment.

> *"People who appear to be all over the place are usually people who have simply not yet connected or made the connection between what they are doing and the purpose of God for their life."*

A marketplace mentality is constantly asking the question: "What else can I do and still be doing what I do?" This may sound like an oddly stated question, but in a couple of paragraphs it will make sense. There are untapped gifts and unrealized opportunities that are in line with your unique assignments that are being activated right now. Resolve to access and release everything that God has blessed you with and say, "I'm going to let God stretch me, and use me wherever God wants to use me in any area of influence on my mountain(s)—not just in a straight line. Whoever is in my reach, I want them to encounter the grace the Lord has put on my life." The Kingdom is advanced as believers live the width of their every ability.

There are two things that are unequivocally true. God has given everyone an assignment and He has given ability to excel in that assignment. With this in mind we understand that people who appear to be all over the place are usually people who have simply not yet connected or made the connection between what they are doing and their God-given assignment. Oftentimes if they are able to find the lowest common denominator (that which all of their interests have in common) and all frustration will be released regarding the specific understanding of God's assignment for their lives.

Earlier I mentioned that as a child I was often in and the winner of, oratorical contests both locally and nationally. In fact, every oratorical contest I was ever in I won! I also was often the lead in school plays. I have been The Nutcracker, Lewis (in the play Lewis and Clark), Papa Bear, Romeo and Walter Lee Younger "Brother" in Raisin in the Sun just to name a few.

Not only that, I was in an independent movie in the late 1980's entitled, "Kiss Grandma Goodbye." In 2012, I was in a Michael Matthews stage play. What is the common denominator in my stage appearances? My assignment as an actor was not just to emote, but also to help my audience experience what the script or screen writer was intending to convey, I had to interpret and express the ideas of someone else.

Additionally, in high school I was president of the student council. At the age of 16, I was elected by my peers to be the first ex-officio member of the Dayton Board of Education. In holding that seat I represented the then nearly 20,000 students in the Dayton Public Schools system. It took the revelation of the Holy Ghost for me to see the commonality between the stage and the boardroom. Even in the innocence and ignorance of my childhood I was being groomed for my unique assignment to be a communicator and a leader to operate on the mountain of arts and entertainment as well as the mountain of religion.

As a leader, I had to bring people together and hold them together for a common cause or goal. Some of the graces I've been gifted with are being a builder of people (disciple maker) and an agent of ideas and information. Now add that to the many leadership roles that God has allowed me to serve in—from the Dayton Board of Education to Pastoring—the picture becomes clearer. Throughout my life, God was shaping me as a Pastor, allowing me to gain experiences that I would later use to build people and make the teaching of the Lord plain to them.

Being a Pastor, leader, teacher and writer, I am operating in different ways, but in essence, I am doing the same things I have always done. Now my script is the scriptures and my stage is the pulpit. As a communicator, now I communicate both verbally and in writing. As a leader, I shape the Biblical worldview of others. Different vehicles fueled by the same abilities I have been in touch with for years.

This is why I say with confidence that God expects us as believers to live the width of every available opportunity. God uses all of our experiences to mold us into His image for our good and for His glory. Romans 8:28-29 says,

> "We are assured *and* know that [God being a partner in their labor] all things work together *and* are [fitting into a plan] for good to *and* for those who love God and are called according to [His] design *and* purpose. For those whom He foreknew [of whom He was aware and loved beforehand], He also destined from the beginning [foreordaining them] to be molded into the image of His Son..." (AMP)

If Jesus had been born and stayed in Mary's house until it was time to go to Calvary, He technically would have fulfilled His burden, fulfilled Old Testament prophecy and secured our salvation. If Jesus had been born and the only thing He did was go to the temple with his Mama, and then went back home, watched the game, then played the Xbox© and PlayStation© all week, and hung out on twitter© and Facebook©, and texted and all that stuff and just went to Calvary, He still would be the Messiah.

But Jesus had a marketplace mentality. Jesus mindset was, "I know there is redemption in me, but I also know there's healing in me." His mindset was, "I know there's salvation in me, but I believe there are miracles in me, also. I know there's restoration in me, but I also believe there's water walking in me. I know I can save humanity, but I also believe I can feed a multitude. I know I can purchase man's salvation, but I also believe I can raise the dead. I know I can die for the sins of the entire world, but I also know I can give sight to the blind. I can give the restoration of hearing to those who are deaf." You and I have not been called to serve just along a straight line; you and I have been called to maximize the entire width of our unique assignment.

Let's be candid, the Kingdom is not advanced by those who live in a straight line. The Kingdom is advanced by those who live large and live at maximum — beyond self-imposed or people imposed boundaries. God is calling and relying on you through the Holy Spirit to dominate this world we live in. The objective is to, in the words of my administrative assistant Demecia Jett, "Apply yourself to the fullest and greatest possible end."

The History Channel's© "The Bible" miniseries is a wonderful example of what happens when believers have a marketplace mentality and live the width of their lives. Passionate Christians, Roma Downey and Mark Burnett seized an opportunity to do something they were familiar with doing already. Tell and produce the most powerful story of all, the story of God! Through the mountain of arts and entertainment they increase the Kingdom of God.

Apple© is yet an even more familiar example of "doing more of what we've already done for the greater good" (their impact being higher profits for their shareholders). What started as a desktop became a laptop, then a phone, then a tablet, then a mini-tablet and only Apple© knows what's next. The shocking reality is as Bishop T.D. Jakes points out, "it's all the same thing." Nevertheless they dominate their market simply by living the width or as my daughter Trinity puts it, "They are doing the most."

Can I tell you what I hear in my spirit right now? I hear, "Eyes have not seen, ears have not heard, neither has it entered into the heart of man what God has in store for you" (1 Cor. 2:9).

The Lord has given you and me authority, and yet He is responsible for making arrangements or creating opportunities for the grace He has placed on our lives. So many times we want to put the arrangements the Lord makes before proper usage of our authority. The yielding of our authority comes before we can appropriately recognize the opportunities created for us. The Lord responds to what we sow. When we sow our authority back into His dominion, the harvest of opportunity (God-orchestrated arrangements) is unlimited.

Remember, it is not the spiritual life that comes first; it is the physical or natural first and then the spiritual. 1 Corinthians 15:45-46 says, "Thus it is written, The first man Adam became a living being (an individual personality); the last Adam (Christ) became a life-giving Spirit [restoring the dead to life].But it is not the spiritual life which came first, but the physical and then the spiritual." (AMP)

You and I doing something natural sets the atmosphere so that God can do something spiritual. You had to naturally pick up this book, so God could do a greater spiritual thing in you. If you didn't naturally do your part, you would have missed what God wants to spiritually do in you. It's natural, and then it's spiritual. God works through your natural circumstances to make spiritual arrangements and create marketplace opportunities.

This is why you cannot get weary in well-doing, because that's when God is working through your natural efforts to cause spiritual arrangements to come to pass for His glory and the good of the Kingdom.

What does this mean? *There are no coincidences in the Kingdom. There are only arrangements in the Kingdom.* Even though the order is natural and then spiritual, spiritual is always the priority that the Lord has in mind.

There is a revelation in 1 Samuel 9. God had a conversation with Samuel about a man named Saul. God told Samuel, "Tomorrow I'm going to send a fellow to you who I want you to anoint as the king of Israel. I've heard the cries of the people, and I'm going to anoint Saul as the king." The next day Saul's father's donkeys got loose. Saul sets out on a mission to find his father's donkeys, not knowing all the time that it really was a spiritual arrangement. While Saul was out looking for donkeys, God had already had a conversation with Samuel about a man coming to him. Sometimes when you think you've experienced loss, it's really not loss; nothing is ever a "loss" in the Kingdom. Sometimes God adds by subtracting and He multiplies by dividing, but nothing is a loss. Once again, this is God working through the natural to cause spiritual arrangements to take place.

> *"God works through the natural to cause spiritual arrangements to take place in our lives."*

In Acts 16, Paul, Silas and Timothy wanted to go to Asia to preach the gospel and the Lord said no. They wanted to go to Bithynia, and the Lord still said no. They ended up in a little place called Troas. When it seems like doors are closed in your face, it may be God working on your behalf making an arrangement for your assignment. It was in Troas that they met a physician named Luke.

We know Paul had an ailment which means he likely needed a physician. Let's assume that Luke most likely treated Paul's ailment. Luke also became Paul's scribe. If Paul didn't have a scribe, he more than likely wouldn't have written the book of Acts. And if we didn't have Acts, we wouldn't know what the first century church was about; neither would we have a picture of the early ministry of the Apostles, the importance of Christian community, Paul's missionary journeys, and so much more. God works through natural situations to cause Kingdom arrangements to come to pass. I've got one more for you.

There is a man named Joseph. In Genesis 50 he testifies, "You meant it for evil, but God meant it for my good." Joseph had no consternation against his brothers for their maliciousness. Instead of being angry, Joseph viewed his brothers' actions as an instrument of the Lord to create an opportunity for a purpose greater than Joseph or his brothers.

The sovereign nature of God has demand on your experiences to set forth the momentum required for the grace He has placed on your life. Believe this for it is true!

Chapter Nine

Yes, It's Personal

We have spent a considerable amount of time examining the call and experience of Jeremiah. It is important that we respect the intensely personal reality of the God and Jeremiah conversation. It's good to hear God talk about others, but it's even better at times to have God talk to you about you. God talks to Jeremiah not only about the nations; God also talks to Jeremiah about himself.

Your marketplace assignment(s) is so personal and important to God that He wants to have an ongoing conversation with you about his plans for your life. There is a particular level of mental toughness that sets in for the believer who engages in dialogue with God concerning their life, anointing and assignment.

Let's look at Jeremiah 1:4-10 again.

> "The word of the LORD came to me, saying, "Before I formed you in the womb I knew you, before you were born I set you apart; I appointed you as a prophet to the nations." "Ah, Sovereign LORD," I said, "I do not know how to speak; I am only a child." But the LORD said to me, "Do not say, 'I am only a child.' You must go to everyone

I send you to and say whatever I command you. Do not be afraid of them, for I am with you and will rescue you," declares the LORD. Then the LORD reached out his hand and touched my mouth and said to me, "Now, I have put my words in your mouth. See, today I appoint you over nations and kingdoms to uproot and tear down, to destroy and overthrow, to build and to plant."

From Genesis to Revelation we see a very particular parallel principle. Wherever there is a parallel principle in scripture that means that principle is going to be applicable at all times, in every situation.

There is one such principle in Genesis 17:1, "When Abram was ninety-nine years old, the Lord appeared to him and said, 'I am the Almighty God; walk *and* live habitually before Me and be perfect [blameless, wholehearted, complete]'" (AMP). Look at what God is doing, He's calling Abram to first set his heart toward Him. He says, "Walk and live habitually before me and be perfect." Look at Exodus 3:10. Exodus 3:10 says, "Come now therefore, and I will send you to Pharaoh, that you may bring forth My people, the Israelites, out of Egypt."

In Genesis 17 God tells Abraham, "Walk before me and be thou perfect." In Exodus 3:10 God tells Moses, "Come now therefore." Matthew 4:18-19: "[18] As He was walking by the Sea of Galilee, He noticed two brothers, Simon who is called Peter and Andrew his brother, throwing a dragnet into the sea, for they were fishermen.[19] And He said to them [what?], Come [come where?] after Me [as disciples—letting Me be your Guide], follow Me, and [what's going to happen?] I will make you fishers of men!"(AMP – emphasis mine).

When we read this text about people being called by God, many times we jump right to what they were being called to do. In the case of the disciples they were called to be fishers of men. However, they were first called to come after Him. This is critical. In fact the success of our marketplace efforts largely rest on understanding that the Lord has a distinctively personal interest in being our Lord and leader above all else. Our personal interaction with Him as such serves as the catalyst for understanding that His mission and our gifts are intricately and divinely connected.

This is why God said to Abraham "I'm your shield and exceeding great reward, but I want you to walk before me (Come after Me)." He says to Peter and Andrew, "Come after Me, I will make you fishers of men. He revealed Himself to Adam in Genesis 2 as LORD God. At the very outset, God established Himself in Adam's life as Adam's priority.

The parallel principle in each of the above references is the principle of alignment. **Core belief #7 – It is the will of God that believers set their hearts _first_ on being in alignment with Him.** Good success demands the order of God first and then all else. The distinguishing word in that sentence is "good".

Only with God can there be good success. If I'm out of alignment, I can't hear from Him or properly see His mission as my mission and my mission as His. It's only when I'm in alignment that I can properly appreciate the synergy that exists between all believers, acknowledge the Lord as being the source of my gifts, celebrate His sovereignty and respect the accou^Intability He demands. We don't miss God because God isn't speaking; we miss God because we fail to maintain the priority He demands and we get out of alignment. God wants you and me to have good success.

Success that is ill gotten or arrived at apart from the influence of Christ and the strength of the Kingdom is not good success. Good success point back to Christ as the reason, for He makes all things concerning life and Godliness possible (2 Peter 1:3).

No matter how non-glamorous or slow your trajectory to good success may be, remember that the Lord has ordained you for excellence. Even if you are running a lemonade stand, know that it would be a lemonade stand like no other in the country. Your marketplace mentality must encourage you to believe that you can work whatever hand has been dealt you. Not just because you're so smart, or you're so wise, but because you're yielding to being aligned with God; seeking after, going after and requiring Him out of necessity.

The secret to success is sanctified surrender. The yielded life is the fruitful life. Mark this revelation, whatever you yield to God He always gives back to you measurably more and qualitatively better than how you gave it to Him. The first act is yielding your right to be selfish and independent. Yield your ways, thoughts, plans, ideas, goals, dreams and ambitions to God. He will see to it that glory rises for Him and growth rises for the Kingdom.

Anybody who has ever sabotaged their assignment has done so in part because of misalignment. This shows up as poor stewardship, lack of sincerity, pride and much more. The Lord requires alignment in all of these areas in order for one to have good success. You must see yourself and every part of your life as God's business! The personal nurturing of your relationship with the Lord is vital to hearing with clarity what the Lord desires for your life.

Here is a natural analogy of the significance and importance of alignment for good success. Consider a fish. Fish can't live outside the water, so there's no reason for a fish to have a vision of dwelling on a mountain. It would die on the mountain. It would be absurd for a fish to be jealous of a bird. Thinking, "I wish I could get up there on that mountain like that bird does" will cost your life, Mr. Fish. Mr. Fish would have to surrender his vision if he is going to have good success. So it is with believers. We must see ourselves as belonging to the Lord first and therefore submitting to His will.

Thinking along these lines calibrates every ambition we have for our own lives and opens our hearts to receive the plan of God to use us on the mountains. Any other way ultimately leads to self-sabotaging.

The goal of every believer ought to be to <u>maintain alignment with God</u>. God must be the principle influence behind how you take care of your health, how you treat your family and how you manage your time and resources. How respond to the mind of God concerning each of these areas is an expression of our alignment.

1 Samuel 15 tells the tragic story of a misaligned man who sabotaged his assignment. Before we look at the text, let me give you the context. God gave King Saul very explicit instructions. "When you go in to take Amalek I want you to kill everybody and everything, including women and children." Why would God tell Saul to kill women and children? That's another lesson altogether. But God says, "Kill all the women, kill all the children, kill the oxen, all the livestock kill everything." In short, Saul is disobedient. Samuel gets a word from the Lord that Saul has not obeyed God. Samuel confronts Saul who denies any wrong doing. Samuel calls this to Saul's attention by saying, "Why do I hear the sheep whining and the oxen bleating?"

Saul sabotaged his assignment because he was aligned with people rather than God. Doing so weakened his sensitivity to hearing from God and heeding to God's promptings. Even when presented with an opportunity to acknowledge his error and repent, he neglected to do so.

When your alignment with God is out of order NOTHING else will work or go well. It's like having an automobile with a wheel misalignment. Washing the car, keeping it garaged, performing cosmetic services on it will not remedy the real problem. Every time you put that car on the road it will pull in one direction more than the other. Ultimately it will impact gas millage, the comfort of the ride and even the way the tires wear on the automobile. The same is true for the believer.

God's feelings about Saul's misalignment is recorded in I Samuel 15:11" I regret making Saul king, for he has turned back from following Me and has not performed My commands. And Samuel was grieved *and* angry [with Saul], and he cried to the Lord all night" (AMP). Look at verse 23. "^For rebellion is as the sin of witchcraft, and stubbornness is as idolatry and teraphim (household good luck images). Because you have rejected the word of the Lord, He also has rejected you from being king" (AMP).

Whenever you think that your way is better than the way of God, you are out of alignment. Rebellion is no small thing; the Lord does not count it such, either. Proverbs 14:12 admonishes us, "There is a way that seems right to a man, but in the end it leads to death."

We have established that critical to hearing the voice of God is the parallel principle of alignment. What are you listening to hear, how does God speak, give instruction and provide clarity? These are matters of grave importance that must be settled in order for us to be clear about our marketplace assignments. After all, the strength of the Kingdom is at stake.

Being in alignment with the Lord is essential to hearing from Him. In order to hear from God, you have to know how God speaks.

Chapter Ten

God Speaks

John 10:4-5 says, "When he has brought his own sheep outside, he walks on before them, and the sheep follow him [why do the sheep follow Him?] because they know his voice. [Know we're tapping into the voice of God, verse 5] They will never [on any account] follow a stranger, but will run away from him because they do not know the voice of strangers *or* recognize their call."(Italics mine.)

Retain this revelation. You don't have to spend a lot of time trying to recognize the voice of the enemy; you just need to invest precious time getting acquainted with the voice of God. The more acquainted you become with the voice of the Lord, the more you'll be able to recognize the trickery of the enemy.

Look at this passage found in II Timothy 3:16-17, "Every Scripture is God-breathed (given by His inspiration) and profitable for instruction, for reproof *and* conviction of sin, for correction of error *and* discipline in obedience, [and] for training in righteousness (in holy living, in conformity to God's will in thought, purpose, and action), [17] So that the man of God may be complete *and* [what?] proficient, well fitted *and* thoroughly equipped for every good work" (AMP).

The voice of God is found primarily in His scripture. God speaks through His Word. God is never going to give you an assignment or lead you to handle your assignment in a way that contradicts His Word. This means you and I have to develop the habit of vetting every thought by the Word of God. It doesn't matter how strongly you feel about something, every thought must pass the "Text Test."

Believer, the Lord will not give you a business plan or urge you to handle a marketplace matter in a way that is a violation of scripture. Even when managing conflict, there is a God honoring way to do so.

The Word of God says it this way, "The weapons we fight with are not the weapons of the world. On the contrary, they have divine power to demolish strongholds. We demolish arguments and every pretension that sets itself up against the knowledge of God, and we take captive every thought to make it obedient to Christ" (II Cor. 10:4-5).

The Lord also speaks through other believers. An example of this is found in I Samuel 3:7-10. "Now Samuel did not yet know the Lord, and the word of the Lord was not yet revealed to him. [8]And the Lord called Samuel the third time. And he went to Eli and said, 'Here I am, for you did call me.' Then Eli perceived that the Lord was calling the boy. [9]So Eli said to Samuel, 'Go, lie down. And if He calls you, you shall say, Speak, Lord, for Your servant is listening.' So Samuel went and lay down in his place. [10]And the Lord came and stood and called as at other times, Samuel! Samuel!' Then Samuel answered, 'Speak, Lord, for Your servant is listening.'"

Samuel's ear had not yet become accustomed to hearing from God. He couldn't discern God yet. So God put Eli in his life to help him identify the voice of God. The Lord will put people in your life that will assist you in discerning Him and His will concerning you.

This is critical to developing a personal hermeneutic supported by the Biblical understanding of knowing the voice of God.

The Word must be the foundation of every believer's core beliefs. We must find our priorities, convictions and boundaries manifested in the Word.

This demands a decisive measure of discipline and repetition. Remember, we are actively pursuing a renewed mind, a mind that thinks beyond Sunday and beyond the sanctuary, a marketplace mentality that reaches and dominates every mountain of heaven and earth. Consistency and discipline are paramount! Hebrews 5:14 gives us the needed revelation on this. It says, "[14] but solid foods is for the mature, who by constant use have trained themselves to distinguish good from evil."

Let's look at I Samuel 3 again, verses 7-10. "Now Samuel did not yet know the Lord, and the word of the Lord was not yet revealed to him. And the Lord called Samuel the third time. And he went to Eli and said, 'Here I am, for you did call me.' Then Eli perceived that the Lord was calling the boy. So Eli said to Samuel, 'Go, lie down. And if He calls you, you shall say, Speak, Lord, for Your servant is listening.' So Samuel went and lay down in his place. And the Lord came and stood and called as at other times, 'Samuel! Samuel!' Then Samuel answered, 'Speak, Lord, for Your servant is listening.'"

Remember, we have established that Samuel's ear had not yet become accustomed to recognizing the voice of God. He couldn't discern God yet and additionally he needed clarity on interpreting the will of God. So, God put somebody in his life to help him identify the voice of God as well as make known the will of God and the mind of God concerning life and his own unique assignment. Keep in mind that this lets us know not only does God speak through the scriptures, He speaks through others.

When God speaks through others, He will affirm, admonish or activate (all of the above or a combination) things concerning your purpose and assignment. However, what is spoken will never contradict His written Word. This cannot be emphasized enough, especially in a day when the marketplace is often overrun by people who lack integrity, character and God consciousness.

The voice of God is heard in the scriptures. The voice of God is heard through others. The voice of God is also heard through your situations.

There are many examples in the scriptures where the plan of God was revealed through particular situations. One example is found in a text we looked at earlier, Acts 16:9-10. Paul desired to visit two other cities to further the Kingdom; during this time he received a vision. The vision Paul received gave him the needed direction he needed concerning what the Lord would have him to do. The Lord spoke to Paul through his situation.

It is needful for the cultivating of a marketplace mentality that this truth is the foundation of our core beliefs and is meditated on often! The Lord desires to minister to you concerning your role in His agenda.

There is a familiar proverb that says "experience is the best teacher". This proverb leans toward the truth but is not entirely true. Experience apart from the Holy Spirit is simply an experience. It is when our experiences are submitted to the wisdom of the Holy Spirit that they become valuable and we can hear God speak. Rom 8:6 provides this truth, "Now the mind of the flesh [which is sense and reason without the Holy Spirit] is death [death that[a]comprises all the miseries arising from sin, both here and hereafter]. But the mind of the [Holy] Spirit is life and [soul] peace [both now and forever]." (AMP)

Please do not allow delay, rejection, hold-ups or setbacks to discourage you. Allow the reality of these situations to make you even more sensitive to the voice of God about His will for your assignment. This level of discipline taps you into the supernatural and it is the supernatural that gives you the edge in your assignment(s).

After reading this book, you have all the required core beliefs you need to embrace, know and live out your role in the advancing of the Kingdom. We have identified the results of assimilating to these core beliefs as being a marketplace mentality. Now, your mission, should you choose to accept it is:

To submit your every gift, skill and ability to the cause of the Kingdom. The Kingdom consists of Arts and Entertainment, Education, Family, Government, Media, Finance and Religion. All of these belong to the Lord. Psalm 24 reminds us, "The earth is the LORD'S, and the fullness thereof; the world, and they that dwell therein"(KJV). Hebrews 2:10 says, "In bringing many sons to glory, it was fitting that God, for whom and through whom everything exists, should make the author of their salvation perfect through suffering."

The culture of the Kingdom must be released over every influence of the world. The enemy has long possessed the Kingdom, influenced the Kingdom and staffed the Kingdom. In fact, in Luke 4:5-6 Satan offers to turn the mountains over. However, his influence was irretrievably compromised on Calvary according to Colossians 2:13-15,

"When you were dead in your sins and in the uncircumcision of your sinful nature, God made you alive with Christ. He forgave us all our sins, having canceled the written code, with its regulations, that was against us and that stood opposed to us; he took it away, nailing it to the cross. And having disarmed the powers and authorities, he made a public spectacle of them, triumphing over them by the cross."

Now it is required of people like you to take your place on the mountains and bring in the inheritance.

This book is only successful if it quickens stirs, activates and awakens something within you that compels you to reclaim your influence, dominate on your mountain(s) and thrusts you into a marketplace mentality.

References

All scripture quoted in this book is from the Holy Bible (public domain), New International Version except where noted.

Preface

1. Billy Sunday. (n.d.). BrainyQuote.com. Retrieved July 25, 2013, from: http://www.brainyquote.com/quotes/quotes/b/billysunda325874.html

Chapter One

2. Marketplace. (n.d.). Retrieved from http://www.merriam-webster.com/dictionary/marketplace
3. McClaren, Brian. 2010. "*A New Kind of Christianity.*" P.18. New York, New York. HarperCollins.
4. Hillman, O.S. (n.d.) Reclaiming the Seven Mountains of Culture. Retrieved from http://www.reclaim7mountains.com/.
5. Bill Winston Ministries. February 26, 2013. [Facebook Update] Retrieved from https://www.facebook.com/billwinstonministries?fref=ts
6. Wallnau, Lance. [Bruce Wilson]. July 16, 2009. Lance Wallnau Explains the Seven Mountain Mandate. [Video File]. Retrieved from http://www.youtube.com/watch?v=qQbGnJd9poc.

7. West, Dr. Cornel. [n.d.] Retrieved from http://www.brainyquote.com/quotes/quotes/c/cornelwest417115.html#YGydTxzBwO-qdELAv.99 .
8. *The New Testament Greek Lexicon.* Strong's Number 1411. Retrieved from www.biblestudytools.com/lexicons/greek/kjv/dunamis.html

Chapter Two
9. Barth, Karl. [n.d.] Retrieved from http://commonquote.com/quote/149741/karl-barth/the-call- -discipleship.

Chapter Three
10. Birth of U.S. Citizens Abroad. [n.d.] Retrieved from http://travel.state.gov/law/family_issues/birth/birth_593.html.

Chapter Five
11. Evans, Dr. Anthony. (2012) *Kingdom Man: Every Man's Destiny, Every Woman's Dream.* Ridgewood, New Jersey. Tyndale House.

Chapter Seven
12. JEHOVAH (YVHV) – Strong's Concordance #03068. Definition – the self-existent one. The proper name of the one true God. This word is unpronounceable. Elohim – (Stong's Concordance #0430, plural intensive–singular meaning) Ruler or judge. Adonai – Strong's Concordance #0113, intensive) Master or Ruler. When written as Jehovah Elohim or Jehovah Adonai it is a superlative that means the God of Gods, the Ruler of Rulers, etc. Retrieved from http://www.biblestudytools.com/lexicons/hebrew/kjv/YVH.html on July 25, 2013.

References

13. Ibid, Retrieved from <http://www.biblestudytools.com/lexicons/hebrew/kjv/adown.html> on July 25, 2013.